THE BEDFORD SERIES IN HISTORY AND CULTURE

Violence in the West

The Johnson County Range War
and the Ludlow Massacre

A BRIEF HISTORY WITH DOCUMENTS

D0107796

Related Titles in
THE BEDFORD SERIES IN HISTORY AND CULTURE
Advisory Editors: Lynn Hunt, *University of California, Los Angeles*
David W. Blight, *Yale University*
Bonnie G. Smith, *Rutgers University*
Natalie Zemon Davis, *Princeton University*
Ernest R. May, *Harvard University*

THE BEDFORD SERIES IN HISTORY AND CULTURE

Violence in the West

The Johnson County Range War and the Ludlow Massacre

A BRIEF HISTORY WITH DOCUMENTS

Marilynn S. Johnson

Boston College

BEDFORD/ST. MARTIN'S   Boston ♦ New York

For Bedford/St. Martin's

Publisher for History: Mary V. Dougherty
Executive Editor: William J. Lombardo
Director of Development for History: Jane Knetzger
Senior Editor: Heidi L. Hood
Developmental Editor: Debra Michals
Editorial Assistant: Katherine Flynn
Production Supervisor: Jennifer Peterson
Executive Marketing Manager: Jenna Bookin Barry
Text Design: Claire Seng-Niemoeller
Project Management: Books By Design, Inc.
Index: Books By Design, Inc.
Cover Design: Joy Lin
Cover Photo: *Armed Coal Miners Assemble outside the San Rafael Hospital in Trinidad, Colorado, as Open Warfare Breaks Out between Strikers, Mine Operators, and National Guard Troops in the Wake of the Ludlow Massacre in 1914.* West Virginia and Regional History Collection, West Virginia University Libraries.
Composition: TexTech International
Printing and Binding: RR Donnelley & Sons Company

President: Joan E. Feinberg
Editorial Director: Denise B. Wydra
Director of Marketing: Karen R. Soeltz
Director of Editing, Design, and Production: Marcia Cohen
Assistant Director of Editing, Design, and Production: Elise S. Kaiser
Manager, Publishing Services: Emily Berleth

Library of Congress Control Number: 2008928038

Manufactured in the United States of America.

3   2   1   0   9   8
f   e   d   c   b   a

For information, write: Bedford/St. Martin's, 75 Arlington Street, Boston, MA 02116   (617-399-4000)

ISBN-10: 0-312-44579-2
ISBN-13: 978-0-312-44579-9

Acknowledgments

Acknowledgments and copyrights appear at the back of the book on page 166, which constitutes an extension of the copyright page.

Distributed outside North America by PALGRAVE MACMILLAN.

Foreword

The Bedford Series in History and Culture is designed so that readers can study the past as historians do.

The historian's first task is finding the evidence. Documents, letters, memoirs, interviews, pictures, movies, novels, or poems can provide facts and clues. Then the historian questions and compares the sources. There is more to do than in a courtroom, for hearsay evidence is welcome, and the historian is usually looking for answers beyond act and motive. Different views of an event may be as important as a single verdict. How a story is told may yield as much information as what it says.

Along the way the historian seeks help from other historians and perhaps from specialists in other disciplines. Finally, it is time to write, to decide on an interpretation and how to arrange the evidence for readers.

Each book in this series contains an important historical document or group of documents, each document a witness from the past and open to interpretation in different ways. The documents are combined with some element of historical narrative—an introduction or a biographical essay, for example—that provides students with an analysis of the primary source material and important background information about the world in which it was produced.

Each book in the series focuses on a specific topic within a specific historical period. Each provides a basis for lively thought and discussion about several aspects of the topic and the historian's role. Each is short enough (and inexpensive enough) to be a reasonable one-week assignment in a college course. Whether as classroom or personal reading, each book in the series provides firsthand experience of the challenge—and fun—of discovering, recreating, and interpreting the past.

Lynn Hunt
David W. Blight
Bonnie G. Smith
Natalie Zemon Davis
Ernest R. May

Preface

For more than a century, popular books and films have portrayed the American frontier as the "Wild West" of marauding desperadoes and gun-toting lawmen. But just how violent was the West, and under what conditions was violence most likely to occur? This volume explores these questions for the late nineteenth and early twentieth centuries through the lens of the dramatic range and mining wars that plagued the region between the 1880s and 1910s, and most specifically through the case studies of the Johnson County range war in Wyoming and the southern Colorado coal strike that culminated in the infamous Ludlow Massacre. Focusing on land use and labor, industrial development, and race and ethnic relations, this volume examines the social conflicts that engulfed the West as an expanding capitalist market transformed the region and ultimately closed the frontier.

The book opens with a general introduction to the topic of western violence, examining the rates and types of violence in different western settings and the social, political, and economic sources of such conflict. While some western communities recorded high rates of interpersonal violence—saloon brawling, street fighting, and the like—others gave rise to episodes of collective violence stemming from larger conflicts over western lands and resources. This was especially true on the ranching and mining frontiers, where a male-dominated population of miners and ranchers clashed with a rising elite that sought to maximize profits by exploiting agricultural, mineral, and labor resources. The introduction traces the history of range and mining disputes in the West and discusses how economic and class conflicts were frequently intertwined with tensions over race, ethnicity, and gender. This section also explores how local and federal authorities sanctioned or intervened in these western "wars" and examines the eventual decline of mass violence in the region.

The second part of the book presents the range and mining wars through a collection of documents that illuminate all sides of the disputes. The first group of documents examines the Johnson County range war, which pitted small ranchers and homesteaders against wealthy cattle owners in northern Wyoming. Documents in this section shed light on the rise and fall of the western cattle boom, the ensuing conflicts over cattle rustling that developed between large and small stock owners, and the use of lynching and hired gunmen that led to a violent standoff between hundreds of armed men in Johnson County in the spring of 1892. Other documents explore the war's aftermath, including the attempted prosecution of the so-called regulators and the federal occupation of Johnson County by African American cavalry troops. Together, these documents highlight the intense conflicts over western land use and the incorporation of the western cattle industry into a larger capitalist market.

The second group of documents chronicles the history of the 1913–1914 coal strike in southern Colorado and the Ludlow Massacre. Illuminating one of the most horrific tragedies in U.S. labor history, the documents in this section look at the origins of the strike, the competing perspectives of the mining company and the union, and the role of state militia and National Guard troops deployed in the strike zone. This section also provides personal accounts of the tragic conflagration that killed more than a dozen men, women, and children at the Ludlow tent camp on April 20, 1914, as well as documents from the ensuing military investigation, all of which offer contrasting perspectives of the events. The documents conclude with an article written by the mining company's leading stockholder, John D. Rockefeller Jr., which inaugurated controversial measures that laid the basis for welfare capitalism — a program of industrial reforms, designed to undercut the appeal of unions, that was widely implemented by U.S. corporations in the 1920s.

The third part of the book, the epilogue, briefly examines how the Johnson County War and the Ludlow Massacre have been remembered by succeeding generations of Americans. Images of the Wild West have been etched in popular memory through music, books, movies, museums, and tourist sites, but some incidents are clearly more resonant than others. This epilogue examines why the Johnson County War has become an important part of our collective memory and cultural history, while the Ludlow Massacre has remained an obscure and embattled chapter of our past.

The format of the book is designed to offer a general framework for understanding the history of western violence and provide specific case studies that allow for more in-depth study and comparison. In addition to the brief introductory discussions that give students important historical background on the conflicts, all of the documents are preceded by short headnotes that identify the author(s), provide historical context, and suggest starting points for interpretation. The book's appendixes include chronologies of events for both the Johnson County War and the Colorado coal strike and a list of questions for consideration to facilitate discussion and class assignments. For those interested in reading more about both cases or the general history of violence in the American West, a selected bibliography is included as well.

ACKNOWLEDGMENTS

The idea for this book came from the students in my western history course at Boston College who have been perennially fascinated by frontier-era violence and its role in American popular culture. Their eagerness to learn more about these conflicts and our lively discussions about related documents convinced me to pursue this project. Although we have never met, Richard Maxwell Brown has long influenced my thinking about violence in the West, and I am indebted to him for providing the analytic groundwork for understanding this issue as part of a larger process of social and economic incorporation. His important books and essays have influenced many historians' works as well as my own. My colleagues and graduate students in Gender, Race, and the Construction of the American West—a course offered through the Boston-area Graduate Consortium in Women's Studies—also provided helpful feedback on early drafts of the introduction and epilogue. Special thanks to Lois Rudnick and Karen Hansen for their thoughtful reading and comments and for our fruitful collaboration and friendship.

The editorial staff at Bedford/St. Martin's has supported this book in myriad ways. Mary Dougherty, Beth Welch, and Jane Knetzger, along with series advisory editor David Blight, helped me frame this project and gave encouragement in the early stages. The reviewers for this volume—Heather Fryer of Creighton University, Peter Rachleff of Macalester College, John Putman of San Diego State University, John Enyeart of Bucknell University, and Phil Roberts of the University of Wyoming—provided useful criticism and suggestions that markedly improved the final product. My developmental editor, Debra Michals, ushered me through the revision and editing process; her sage advice and enthusiastic support have made for a far better book. Katherine Flynn provided important legwork and assistance in the final stages of manuscript preparation, and Barbara Jatkola provided meticulous copyediting. I owe all these scholars and editors a debt of gratitude.

Finally, my family—Dan, Rosa, and Jacob—gave me the time to work on this book, distracted me from it when needed, and generally kept me going with their love, care, and patience.

Marilynn S. Johnson

Contents

Illustrations

PART ONE

Introduction:
The American West:
A Violent Land?

Every summer night in Deadwood, South Dakota, visitors gather on Main Street to watch Judge William Kuykendall shoot it out with wanted killer Jack McCall. Most of these tourists have already visited Old Style Saloon #10, a historic restoration of the watering hole where McCall allegedly shot Wild Bill Hickok as he played poker one night in 1876. Three times a day at the #10, visitors can witness a reenactment of McCall's killing of Hickok, the legendary lawman of Abilene, Kansas. And each evening, they can watch the murder trial of McCall, who was shot and captured by Judge Kuykendall, reenacted in the nearby Masonic temple. Except for the actual hanging of McCall, every facet of the case is depicted in violent and painstaking detail, serving as the theme for Deadwood's numerous saloons, casinos, and other tourist attractions. The 2004 premier of the popular HBO series *Deadwood* further fueled the town's booming tourism.

Deadwood is one of several western towns that draws on its frontier heritage of violent conflict to attract tourism and boost the local economy. As in Tombstone, Arizona; Dodge City, Kansas; and other former frontier outposts, the towns' entrepreneurs have discovered what book publishers and movie producers have long known: Western violence sells. But the commercial appeal builds on a deeper mythology of western violence dating back more than 150 years. Nineteenth-century chroniclers of the West immortalized the heroic frontiersmen who fought Indians, hunted wild animals, and captured outlaws. Their work epitomized the western struggle against nature and savagery, a violent battle that could help rejuvenate a sickly eastern civilization beset by urbanization, industrialization, immigration, and labor unrest. Promoted by popular dime novelists of the 1860s, as well as by more elite figures such as the artist Frederic Remington and President Theodore Roosevelt in the 1890s, the glorification of western violence has long been a pervasive feature of western history, art, and literature.[1]

But the question remains: Just how violent was the West in reality? There is no simple answer, because the levels and types of violence varied according to the local economy and culture. Some parts of the trans-Mississippi West, particularly the farming frontier, produced many peaceful cooperative communities. The influence of religion and culture was important in these places. The relatively homogeneous communities of Norwegians on the Great Plains and German Hutterites in the Dakotas and Montana were examples of more harmonious frontier societies. The Wild West in these areas was not so wild after all. But in other parts of the region, notably the Sierra Nevada and Rocky Mountain mining frontiers and the rangelands of the western Great Plains and Great Basin, violent conflict was common. It is these areas that have given the West its rough-and-rowdy reputation.

Scholars have identified at least three types of violent conflict that prevailed in the region: personal, collective, and state-sanctioned warfare. Personal violence between individuals—including assault, murder, suicide, rape, and violent robbery or vandalism—is the most common and is generally classified as criminal behavior. Group or collective violence can take many forms, but in the frontier West, it was mainly manifested as organized banditry, lynching, and vigilante actions. Beginning with the Spanish conquest and culminating in the Indian wars of the late nineteenth century, state-sanctioned warfare was also a critical factor in western expansion. To assess the relative levels of violence in the West, then, each form of conflict must be examined more closely.

Historians agree that western wars of conquest were bloody. White settlers' accounts have emphasized the terror of Indian attacks and scalpings and the taking of captives—all of which occurred with some regularity in the nineteenth century. But in the long run, it was Native Americans who bore the brunt of the violence through battles with the U.S. military, forced marches, dispossession of their homelands, and incarceration in prisons and reservations. Although epidemic disease had the most devastating impact on native populations, warfare also took its toll. Young male warriors accounted for many of the casualties, but the military periodically punished marauding Indian bands by attacking peaceful encampments of women and children. In 1864, for instance, the Colorado militia retaliated against Indian raids on white miners and emigrants by massacring 200 Cheyenne and Arapaho men, women, and children camped along Sand Creek. Other massacres followed: The army killed more than 100 Cheyenne on the Washita River in Oklahoma in 1868, some 170 Blackfeet along the Marias River in Montana in 1870, and more than 150 Sioux in the 1890 massacre at Wounded Knee, South Dakota. Indian deaths often continued after military defeat. The Cherokee, Nez Perce, Paiute, and other groups were forced to endure long marches off their homelands under brutal conditions or died of disease or neglect in military prisons and on reservations. The combined impact of war and disease devastated the native population, which fell from an estimated 600,000 in 1800 to only 250,000 by the 1890s.[2]

Warfare also proved costly for Hispanics in the Southwest. Hundreds of soldiers, Mexican and Anglo, perished in the Texas rebellion of 1836 and the Mexican-American War of 1846–1848. The Texas conflict was especially brutal. More than six hundred men died at the Alamo when the Mexican general Antonio López de Santa Anna ordered a siege and assault on the mission. A few months later, Santa Anna executed some three hundred U.S. prisoners who surrendered during the battle at Goliad. "Remember the Alamo" and "Remember Goliad" became rallying cries for U.S. troops who later conquered Texas and parts of Mexico in the Mexican-American War. Both conflicts were short-lived, but Tejanos (Texans of Mexican descent) endured continuing violence and land dispossession by Anglos, as did the Hispanic residents of California. This legacy of conquest produced deep-seated racial and ethnic resentments between whites and Mexicans that would generate future conflicts and violence in the region.

Although the conquest of native and Hispanic America produced the highest levels of violence and killing in the West, sporadic frontier violence continued for decades as white (and nonwhite) newcomers contended with one another over the future of the region. Their conflicts took personal and collective forms. The lack of consistent data makes it virtually impossible to assess personal violence and violent crime in the West over time. Attempts to compare modern FBI crime statistics to nineteenth-century arrest rates in frontier towns, for example, are highly problematic. Crime statistics mean little in the absence of population figures. Modern crime statistics are measured per 100,000 people, but highly mobile frontier populations fluctuated wildly and were rarely counted accurately. Moreover, frontier law enforcement was hardly comparable to today's urban police forces, which are far more likely to detect, record, and solve crimes. Even the definitions of what constitutes criminal behavior have changed. Some forms of fighting and even killing (lynching, for example) were tolerated in many frontier settings and may not have been reported as criminal offenses.

One way to avoid some of these pitfalls is to concentrate on homicide statistics recorded by local coroners. Historians of crime have found homicide records to be a fairly reliable indicator of lethal violence, since most localities systematically recorded nonaccidental killings (including lynchings and other killings that might not appear in police or court records). Coroners' inquests and death certificates have been standard features of American jurisprudence for centuries, thus allowing for comparisons across time. In at least two studies of western boomtowns in the late nineteenth and early twentieth centuries, historians found markedly high rates of homicide. One study of mining and cattle towns in Nebraska, Colorado, and Arizona from 1880 to 1920 found homicide rates ranging from 6 to 70 per 100,000, well above the rates of New York, Boston, and Philadelphia in the same period, all of which hovered below 5 per 100,000. Another study of Aurora and Bodie, two California gold mining towns in the 1860s to 1880s, revealed homicide rates of 64 and 116 per 100,000, respectively. These rates were not only high by nineteenth-century standards, but they exceed the recent 40 to 56 per 100,000 rates of murder-prone capitals such as New Orleans, Baltimore, and Washington, D.C.[3]

Historians attribute these high rates of homicide to rowdy and drunken behavior by young armed men in the streets, saloons, and residences of western towns. Rapid population growth and turnover, economic booms and busts, racial and ethnic diversity, and high rates of gun ownership and alcohol use all contributed to a volatile social climate. Many murders began with minor arguments over card games, women, or even "too much foam on the beer" and then escalated into knife fights or gunfights. Others resulted from domestic disputes or conflicts between police and those they were trying to arrest. The laws of western states, which increasingly abandoned the common-law requirement that citizens retreat from violent threats, encouraged many combatants to stand their ground with fists and weapons.[4] Racial tensions also played a role in fueling hostilities, but typically all-white juries were more likely to convict African Americans, Hispanics, and Native Americans for the homicides that resulted.

The prevalence of other violent crimes such as armed robbery, rape, arson, and burglary is much harder to assess. One historian, echoing contemporary views of the National Rifle Association, argues that property crime rates in the frontier West were markedly lower than they are today because an armed citizenry served as a deterrent.[5] However, the crime statistics on which such conclusions are based are questionable. The low numbers of rapes noted in some western towns may be due more to low reporting rates and characteristically smaller female populations. Moreover, rapes of Native American and Mexican women as well as prostitutes were probably not considered criminal offenses and were likely not recorded. In both cases, the sexual immorality and availability of such women was taken for granted. Unless allied with police or pimps or married to white men, these women did not benefit from male protection against violence.

Gender is an important key to understanding variations in patterns of western violence. The raucous mining and ranching frontiers had an abundance of young single men, who have throughout history accounted for a disproportionate share of homicides and violence. While some point to men's biology—chromosomes and hormones—as determining aggressive male behavior, cultural factors such as honor codes were likely more important. Honor systems that required men to stand up to challenges or insults through physical action typically flourished in rural societies such as the Old South and may have been transported to the West by southern emigrants. Whatever its origins, the "Code of the West" became a recognized tenet that called on men to redress grievances and defend their reputations by any means necessary. Honor systems were hardly unique to Anglo-American men. Earlier Hispanic settlers transported Mediterranean honor codes to the American Southwest, and some Native American warrior cultures emphasized courage, physical prowess, and violence to avenge attacks on their families and clans. The validation of courage and vengeance, combined with abundant guns and alcohol, proved a lethal mix in male-dominated mining and ranching areas.[6]

By contrast, family groups dominated the relatively placid farming frontier and quickly produced a more balanced sex ratio. Moreover, as the number of women and families increased, western communities established schools, churches, and other institutions that facilitated social order. White women were often characterized as "civilizers" who "tamed" the West by transplanting a refined, domesticated Victorian culture. This gendered view was first immortalized in Owen Wister's 1902 novel *The Virginian* and has been reproduced in western novels and films ever since.

Such a stereotypical view of western women as "gentle tamers" overlooks the ways in which women were sometimes implicated in class and racial animosities. As in the nineteenth-century South, the protection of white womanhood in the West often became an excuse for violence among men. In San Francisco and other western cities, vigilante movements justified their violence in the name of protecting women and children from boomtown crime and vice. In some cases, women incited mob action in defense of maternal and familial values. In Clifton and Morenci, Arizona, Anglo women outraged over the adoption of white orphans by Mexican mining families in 1904 convinced their husbands to organize a posse and forcibly seize the children.[7] In other mining communities, Hispanic and immigrant women united around fathers and husbands, supporting their strike efforts in the face of violence and death. For instance, an elderly labor leader known as Mother Jones rallied hundreds of miners to resist armed guards and federal troops during the 1914 coal miners' strike in Colorado (Document 22). Depending on the context, women could either encourage a stable family and community life or play a role in frontier tensions and violence.

While the levels of personal violence in the West varied, incidents of collective violence were widespread between 1850 and 1920. Organized group violence took two forms: outlaw activity and vigilante action, both of which flourished in frontier areas. Horse thieves, highwaymen, and cattle rustlers were scourges of western life that floated easily around the sparsely settled countryside, evading local law enforcement. In some cases, such outlaw activity was politically motivated. Common people sometimes resisted elite domination through acts of theft, vandalism, and physical intimidation and violence. Historians refer to such individuals as "social bandits"—Robin Hood–type figures who enjoyed popular support as they plundered banks, railroads, large ranches, and other symbols of wealth and power. Resentful of elites' consolidation of local land, labor, and resources, workers and small property owners often proved sympathetic to social bandits. Some, such as Jesse James, Billy the Kid, and Juan Cortina, even became western folk heroes. If local law enforcement was unable or unwilling to curb outlaw bands, elite westerners either hired gunmen and private detectives to protect their interests or organized vigilante movements to hunt down the offenders.

Vigilantism was a widespread American phenomenon that flourished particularly under rural or frontier conditions. Beginning with the regulators of upcountry South Carolina in the 1760s, frontier elites organized vigilante movements to punish crime and immorality and reassert an older vision of social order. Calling themselves regulators, white caps, or vigilance committees, these groups proliferated on the trans-Appalachian frontier prior to the Civil War and sprang up west of the Mississippi River in the second half of the nineteenth century. Between 1850 and 1902, there were more than two hundred organized vigilante movements in the trans-Mississippi West, with particularly high concentrations in California, Montana, and Texas. Except for Utah and Oregon, every western state or territory documented significant vigilante activity. Of the 729 vigilante killings recorded nationwide from 1767 to 1902, western groups were responsible for more than 70 percent. Of the nation's ten most deadly vigilante groups in American history, seven were located in western states or territories.[8]

Frontier areas provided fertile ground for vigilante movements because of the weakness of state-sanctioned law enforcement. In sparsely settled areas, there were neither the tax revenues nor the infrastructure to support a regular police and court system. County sheriffs were usually based in large towns and had few resources for pursuing more mobile lawbreakers. Moreover, inadequate funding also resulted in unsuccessful prosecutions and poorly constructed jails that were easy to escape from. In the absence of effective law enforcement, prominent citizens organized vigilante groups to hunt and punish criminals. Many groups adopted a military organization, had bylaws or constitutions, and held impromptu trials for their victims—who were almost always convicted and executed. The elite leadership and the use of conventional structures and legal rituals suggest that such groups had considerable legitimacy, most likely rooted in the notion of popular sovereignty—the right of the people to rule themselves—that dated back to Revolutionary times. In fact, some vigilante movements referred to themselves as "revolutionary tribunals" and defended their actions as "self-preservation" and protection of property. For these groups, upholding the social order by taking the law into their own hands was a patriotic duty, and prominent statesmen from Andrew Jackson to Theodore Roosevelt applauded their efforts. Americans' suspicion of centralized power and the decentralized nature of the state also contributed to a penchant for vigilantism. Indeed, there was no significant vigilante tradition in the British Isles, nor was there much extralegal activity in western Canada or Mexico, where federal police forces (the Mounties and the Federales) took responsibility for capturing outlaws.[9]

While popular sovereignty justified vigilantism in the absence of local law enforcement, it could also sanction extralegal action when police and court systems were established and functioning—but not to the satisfaction of local elites. In gold rush San Francisco, for example, the Vigilance Committees of 1851 and 1856 bypassed the Irish-dominated police department and courts and executed eight suspects, many of whom were immigrants or nonwhite. Likewise, as will become clear in part two, there was a well-established legal system in Johnson County, Wyoming, in 1892, but its actions and decisions infuriated the state's large cattle owners. In such cases, vigilantes claimed that the legal system was ineffective or corrupt, and just as the American colonists had rebelled against British rule, westerners rationalized taking the law into their own hands when the state tolerated (or perhaps encouraged) anarchy and disorder.

Collective violence and vigilantism, combined with state-sanctioned warfare against Native Americans, contributed to the West's reputation for violence and brutality after the Civil War. Historian Richard Maxwell Brown offers a useful perspective for understanding this pervasive violence, arguing that such conflicts must be seen in the context of the capitalist development and incorporation of the West. From the 1850s through World War I, the West experienced dozens of wars and violent uprisings that Brown calls the "western civil wars of incorporation." On one side of these wars were Native Americans and Hispanic settlers, Anglo homesteaders, immigrant wageworkers, and other smallholders who earned modest livelihoods from western lands and resources. On the other were wealthy and powerful individuals and companies that sought to incorporate these same lands and resources into a national and international market economy. In many rural areas, the incorporators—railroads, land companies, and large ranching, mining, and timber interests—carried out what was in effect a land-enclosure movement. Their efforts to incorporate western lands and resources inspired resistance by the dispossessed and by small operators, who challenged their dominance. In urban areas, incorporating interests hired gunmen and vigilante groups to maintain a version of law and order that was conducive to their business interests. Dangerous or disruptive social behavior, including strikes and labor unrest, was firmly suppressed.[10]

Like the American Civil War, which pitted the forces of Northern free labor against a Southern society based on slavery and plantation agriculture, the western civil wars of incorporation were a set of contests between different modes of capitalist development. In the West, though, a rising group of large-scale capitalists squared off against smaller, more independent or upstart interests. In many disputes, the incorporators—often northern Republicans—enjoyed close ties to state and federal officials and could enlist their support. The resisters—often Democrats, Populists, or labor radicals—generally fought a rearguard action with broad local support. While some of the resisters were explicitly anticapitalist, most embraced an older vision of independent labor and landholding that is sometimes known as producerism. These small producers battled large capitalist incorporators but feared those at the bottom of society who might be deployed against them. In a few cases, Chinese and Mexican strikebreakers or black soldiers got caught in the cross fire when incorporators tapped them to replace or subdue the resisters.[11]

Over time, the locus of the western civil wars of incorporation shifted. Violent conflict between the U.S. government and Native Americans ended in 1890, when the last of the Sioux were defeated and confined to reservations. Anglo and Hispanic westerners continued to fight over control of the rangelands, but these battles gradually gave way to the more urban-centered mining wars and labor conflicts that swept the region after 1890. This collection examines the latter two types of conflict through case studies of the Johnson County range war in Wyoming in 1892 and the Colorado coal strike of 1913–1914, which culminated in mass violence at Ludlow. Both incidents were part of a larger national struggle in the late nineteenth and early twentieth centuries between rising capitalist interests on the one hand and restive workers and agrarian populists who defied their power on the other. In the waning days of the western frontier, this struggle was especially bitter, as the outcome would determine who would control the West for the foreseeable future. To understand these incidents, we must first explore the history of these regions and the varieties of social conflict that flourished there.

THE RANGE WARS

From Kansas cattle towns to the high chaparral of the Sierra Nevada, the violence of the ranching frontier was legendary, and for good reason. With so many competing enterprises, social groups, and land use practices, the pastoral West witnessed numerous gunfights and range wars and much vigilante violence in the late nineteenth century. Although most of this violence amounted to skirmishing rather than all-out war, these conflicts reflect the contentious social and economic relations of this environmentally fragile region.

While the 1880s and 1890s were the peak years of conflict on the western ranges, the origins of this conflict date back to the rise of the cattle industry in the mid-nineteenth century. The cattle business began on a small scale along the overland trails in the 1840s and 1850s as traders bought tired and footsore oxen from passing emigrants and then rested and fattened them for resale. But the roots of the large-scale cattle industry lay farther south, where Texan ranchers took Spanish criollo stock and bred it with English Herefords, producing the hardy Texas longhorn. The longhorn proliferated as beef demand grew, particularly during the Civil War when access to Union and Confederate beef markets was temporarily closed off in the West. After the war, Jesse Chisholm and other Texas cattlemen organized "long drives" to transport the herds to railroad shipping points in Kansas, where they would be loaded onto trains bound for the Chicago slaughterhouses. Rowdy cattle towns developed in places such as Abilene, Ellsworth, and Dodge City. Over the next twenty years, more than two million head of cattle would be driven up the trails to meet the booming market for beef among Americans back east.

As agricultural settlement crept westward across Kansas, however, the cattle industry met its first big obstacle: farmers and homesteaders. Raising livestock along with crops, the newcomers saw their Anglo-American cows succumb to Texas fever, a fatal cattle disease transmitted by ticks that were carried by the longhorns (which were themselves immune to the disease). As the drives moved into Kansas, settlers guarded their property with rifles to prevent the Texas cattle from coming too close and infecting their herds. Before long, the farmers predominated, and one town after another banned the drives. At the same time, however, railroads expanded across Wyoming, Colorado, and Montana, providing new shipping points farther west, away from agricultural settlement.[12] Cattlemen also discovered that if herds wintered on northern ranges, the disease dissipated (because the ticks died at colder temperatures). Moreover, the burgeoning railroad camps, military forts, and Indian reservations of the Rocky Mountain region provided new western markets for the beef industry. Seizing these opportunities, Charles Goodnight, Oliver Loving, and other Texas cattlemen moved herds up to the northern ranges in the 1870s.

By the late 1870s and 1880s, the cattle industry was booming in western Nebraska and the eastern plains of Wyoming, Colorado, and Montana. Texas cattle kings also moved herds into New Mexico and Arizona, while eastern-bred cattle from Oregon expanded along the Columbia Plateau. With low start-up expenses and seemingly unlimited free grass on the open range, European and eastern capital flooded the region, expanding the herds at an astonishing rate. By the mid-1880s, there were an estimated 7.5 million head of cattle on the Great Plains north of Texas, and millions more on the southwest and northwest ranges. As the number of cattle grew, arid western ranges were soon overstocked and overgrazed. By the early 1880s, it took ten to twenty times more land to support a steer on the western plains as it had in 1870.

Disaster ensued when severe winters and drought struck the region from 1885 to 1887. A series of hot, dry summers left the overgrazed land in poor condition and the cattle thin and weakened. The summer drought was punctuated by relentless winter storms that froze the herds against fence lines and sent others into nearby towns in pain and hunger. Millions of cattle perished, with losses averaging 30 percent on the northern plains (as high as 85 percent in the hardest-hit areas). Surprisingly, the massive losses did not result in increased beef prices. Instead, wary creditors called in their loans, forcing cattle owners to sell many of the surviving animals in a glutted market, driving prices even lower. Across the plains, outside investors cut their losses and pulled out, while the remaining ranchers confronted bankruptcy or financial setbacks. In the wake of this disaster, ranchers guarded their investments more closely, streamlining their operations and fighting any threats to their interests. Through statewide stock growers associations, large cattle owners consolidated their control of the industry by regulating its membership and business practices, often with the sanction of state governments. They did so partly in response to competitive threats from small ranchers and homesteaders who challenged their supremacy.[13]

Under the Homestead Act of 1862, which offered 160 acres of government land to those willing to live on and develop their claims, a wave of new settlers moved to the Great Plains after the Civil War. In 1877, the Desert Land Act granted even larger homesteads to those willing to irrigate and farm the arid lands of the western Great Plains and Great Basin. While some farmed, the arid climate west of the ninety-eighth meridian (which averaged less than twenty inches of rainfall annually) convinced many settlers to take up cattle or sheep raising. By the 1880s, the newcomers' small herds were putting further pressure on the overstocked ranges and intermixing with the larger—and often better quality—herds of the cattle kings. Taking up claims along the river valleys, some homesteaders put up fences, cutting off cattlemen's access to watering holes and sheltered winter pastures. To protect their access to rangelands and water, large cattle operators used many tactics. Some bought the land outright; others had their families and employees file homestead claims around key water sources, thus capturing the surrounding range for their exclusive use. In some cases, ranchers built barbed-wire fences around their customary ranges, closing off large sections of the public domain. When the large cattle owners controlled local politics— which they often did—legal challenges to these practices were rarely successful.

Small ranchers fought back in extralegal ways. In the Texas Panhandle, smallholders engaged in a fence-cutting war in 1883–1884, removing barbed wire to give their animals access to public grazing lands. Fence cutting was also a common tactic in New Mexico in the 1890s, where cattle and sheep owners struggled to retain access to customary grazing lands claimed by large landholders. In Wyoming, Texas, and other areas, smallholders struck back by rustling (or claiming) stray unbranded calves or stealing branded steers and horses. While the rustling of mavericks (unbranded cattle) had been a customary right among cowboys, large stock owners clamped down on it as their financial situation tightened in the 1880s. The cattlemen's associations hired stock detectives to hunt rustlers and organized vigilantes to lynch offenders. Granville Stuart led such a group in Montana in 1884, killing more than a hundred horse thieves and range squatters.[14] Eight years later, the Wyoming Stock Growers Association organized a similar campaign with the support of the state government, sparking the Johnson County War.

THE JOHNSON COUNTY WAR

Located in north-central Wyoming, the area known as Johnson County begins at the crest of the Bighorn Mountains, slopes east through forests and canyons, and stretches out through rolling grasslands and sagebrush surrounding the Powder River. In the mid-nineteenth century, these lands were prime buffalo hunting grounds for the Lakota Sioux. In the 1860s, white travelers bound for the Montana goldfields opened the Bozeman Trail through the area, where their growing presence sparked numerous conflicts with the Sioux and other Plains tribes. The U.S. Army built several forts to provide protection, including Fort McKinney in 1876 at the conclusion of Indian-white hostilities in the area. The new frontier town of Buffalo sprouted up nearby. When the county was officially organized in 1881, it contained only a few hundred white inhabitants, most of whom serviced and supplied the fort.

That year saw the first large cattle herds driven up from Texas. Moreton Frewen, a wealthy British landowner, was the first to set up a large-scale ranching operation in Johnson County, but Horace Plunkett and other eager investors from the East Coast and the British Isles followed. By the early 1880s, there were approximately 200,000 head of cattle grazing the Powder River ranges. Many owners of large cattle outfits were absent most of the year, their day-to-day affairs run by local ranch foremen who supervised dozens of cowhands. In 1879, the cattle "barons," as the large stock owners came to be called, organized the Wyoming Stock Growers Association (WSGA) to advance their economic and political interests.[15] The association registered brands, organized spring roundups, and lobbied state government.

As the Wyoming ranges filled with livestock, the WSGA instigated rules to protect the interests of large growers and thwart new competitors. In 1884, the association began prohibiting members from employing cowboys who owned cattle or brands because they feared that these men would claim the stray, unbranded calves of their owners—a practice known as mavericking. Moreover, that year the WSGA pushed a bill through the territorial legislature requiring that all mavericks be rounded up, branded, and auctioned by the association, with the proceeds used for hiring stock detectives to apprehend thieves. Only WSGA members in good standing could bid on mavericks. By vesting these powers in the association, the Wyoming legislature gave it quasi-governmental status.

In 1885 and 1886, a series of dry summers and hard winters put additional pressure on the overgrazed ranges, resulting in falling cattle prices and financial losses for cattle companies, who then laid off some of their cowhands. The WSGA responded by getting its members to abolish free winter meals for cowhands and cut their wages by five dollars a month. To discourage rustling, it also prohibited stock owning by cowboys employed by WSGA members. When such measures took effect in the spring of 1886, cowboys in Johnson County organized a strike and convinced employers to restore their wages. The cowboys' victory was short-lived, as the harsh winter of 1886–1887 killed thousands of cattle and devastated the industry. By spring, many companies had gone out of business, and scores of cowboys had been laid off.

Some of the former cowboys filed homesteads in the area and set out to build small ranches of their own. They joined a growing population of homesteaders who had taken up plots along the Powder River. Mostly, they raised small herds of livestock, grazing them on nearby ranges. The cattlemen resented the newcomers, who competed with them for water and dwindling grasses. Big stock growers particularly resented the "rustlers" who stole their unbranded calves off the open range, a practice they believed was crippling their business. In fact, most homesteaders ran legitimate operations, but a small number did steal. Sometimes it was hard to tell the difference. A good example was the ranch run by James Averell and Ellen Watson (Figure 1) in nearby Carbon County. In 1889, suspected of receiving stolen cattle, the couple was kidnapped and lynched, which outraged many local residents but was condoned by most big stock growers.

As tensions grew between cattlemen and smallholders, the WSGA pressed the state legislature (Wyoming was admitted to the union in 1890) to pass a second antimavericking bill in 1891. The law authorized the new Wyoming Livestock Commission, dominated by WSGA members, to seize and impound the cattle of suspected rustlers. Soon after, five railroad carloads of cattle were confiscated. Bills of sale were not accepted as proof of ownership, and appeals to state authorities were generally ignored. That fall, outraged small cattle operators in Johnson County united to form a competing organization called the Northern Wyoming Farmers and Stock Growers Association. Two of their supporters, Orley E. "Ranger" Jones and John A. Tisdale, were soon ambushed and killed outside Buffalo, reportedly by former county sheriff and stock detective Frank Canton. Anger over the killings fueled growing enthusiasm for the new organization, and in defiance of WSGA regulations, the group announced that it would hold a separate roundup the following April, a month prior to the WSGA roundup. The cattle operators vowed to stop it and began recruiting hired gunmen from Texas.

On April 5, 1892, just before the April roundup, a train carrying fifty men and three cars of horses left the Cheyenne station heading northwest. Calling themselves "regulators," the group was commanded by Major Frank Wolcott, a Civil War veteran and manager of a large ranching operation in southern Wyoming. They debarked at Casper

Figure 1. *Ellen Watson, aka "Cattle Kate"*

Ellen Watson, also known as "Cattle Kate," was a homesteader on prime land located along the Sweetwater River in Carbon County, Wyoming. In the summer of 1889, she and her husband, James Averell, were lynched by a group of local residents who accused them of cattle rustling.

Wyoming State Archives, Department of State Parks and Cultural Resources.

early the next morning, saddled up, and set off for Johnson County with a list of seventy alleged rustlers to be hunted down and executed. On April 9, the regulators surrounded a cabin at the KC Ranch, where Nate Champion, a foreman in the unauthorized roundup, and three other men were staying. When Champion's associate, Nick Ray, left the house to get firewood, the regulators opened fire and killed him. Champion pulled Ray's body back inside and exchanged fire with the regulators for hours. Later that afternoon, the regulators set the cabin on fire and killed Champion in a hail of bullets as he fled.

Learning that angry residents in Buffalo had formed a posse to arrest them, the regulators took refuge at the TA Ranch, a few miles to the north, on April 10. The next day, a posse of three hundred local settlers surrounded the ranch buildings occupied by the regulators. Buffalo merchants donated weapons and ammunition to the posse, while local women cooked meals and sent them by wagon to the TA. A two-day standoff ensued, as both sides dug in behind defensive breastworks and traded gunfire. Two men were killed in the fighting. Once word of the siege at the TA Ranch reached Acting Governor Amos Barber, a Republican political ally of the WSGA, he telegraphed Washington for help in putting down an "insurrection" in Johnson County. On April 13, President Benjamin Harrison (also a Republican) dispatched roughly one hundred troops from Fort McKinney to the TA Ranch. They quickly placed the regulators in custody and escorted them to Fort McKinney.

Before long, however, Governor Barber ordered that the regulators be moved out of Johnson County, arguing that they were in danger. Most Johnson County residents, who wanted the regulators to be tried by a local jury for the killing of Champion and Ray, were outraged. The prisoners were taken to Fort D. A. Russell outside Cheyenne, the state capital and headquarters of the WSGA. As close associates of the judge and other state officials, the stockmen and their hired men were permitted to move freely about town and carry weapons; some even bragged openly of organizing another mission to Johnson County. Amid rumors of another "invasion," Johnson County remained in a state of fear and witnessed a wave of retaliatory violence and vandalism. Several large ranches were looted or burned, and a U.S. deputy marshal aligned with the stock growers was murdered that May.

In early June, the cattlemen called on the governor and federal officials to declare martial law and send additional troops. Displeased with the Sixth Cavalry at Fort McKinney because of the troops' friendly relations with local residents, cattle operators urged federal officials to send the all-black Ninth Cavalry, saying that "the colored troops will have no sympathy for Texan thieves." Less than a week later, President Harrison dispatched the Ninth Cavalry, whose members were known as buffalo soldiers, to Suggs, Wyoming, a railroad camp north of Johnson County. Local settlers' antipathy toward federal troops dispatched to protect big cattle owners, combined with long-standing racial animosity toward the buffalo soldiers, quickly sparked violence. On June 17, a gunfight between soldiers and townspeople in Suggs left one soldier dead and two wounded. This was the last of several deaths resulting from the Johnson County War, but passions surrounding the dispute would resonate through western politics, society, and popular culture for generations.[16]

Ultimately, no one was ever tried or convicted for the Johnson County violence and killings. After four months, the regulators were released on their own recognizance, and following protracted disputes over jury selection, their cases were dismissed in January 1893. One of the conflict's immediate effects was a political rebellion against the state's Republican leadership in the 1892 election, as Governor Barber and Wyoming senators Francis Warren and Joseph Carey were ousted by Democratic challengers. The state's big cattle owners continued to strike back against alleged rustlers by hiring private detectives and gunmen to hunt them down. Increasingly, though, they targeted sheep owners, who by the 1890s were moving in large numbers onto the western rangelands. Although some cattle owners also owned sheep, most were adamantly opposed to these animals, which they believed damaged the range and made it unfit for cattle. When boundary markers or lawsuits failed to keep sheep off the range, cattlemen turned to violence. From the Tonto Basin in Arizona to the Columbia Plateau in Oregon, cattlemen battled sheep owners by running their herds off cliffs or into rivers, shooting at herders, and burning their camps. Between the 1880s and the early 1900s, thousands of sheep were destroyed or run off and several herders injured or killed. Race, religion, and class played a significant role in these sheep-cattle conflicts, as many of the targeted sheep owners and herders were poorer Hispanics, Basques, and Mormons.

Although both the poor and the wealthy relied on vigilantism and other extralegal measures, a class dynamic characterized most range wars. Nearly all of these conflicts pitted a wealthy cattle-owning elite against a larger group of small ranchers, sheepherders, or homesteaders. In some cases, the battle between big and small operators was complicated by other factors that could produce regional cross-class alliances. In the Texas fence-cutting war of the 1880s, for example, the New York and Texas Land Company made big profits selling land to homesteaders and hence supported their fence-cutting campaigns against cattle kings. In New Mexico, ethnic and cultural ties led some wealthy Hispanic ranchers to side with poor villagers in protecting customary land grants. Range wars were thus not simply expressions of class conflict but also were affected by race, culture, and competing economic alliances. Understanding their origins helps us to see western violence as part of a larger national struggle over land, labor, and capitalist development in nineteenth-century America.

THE MINING WARS

While some westerners sought wealth or economic independence through stock raising, others turned to prospecting and mining in hopes of striking it rich. Beginning with the California gold rush of 1849, thousands of emigrants flooded the West seeking gold and other precious metals. Along with the deluge from the eastern states, gold seekers came from as far away as Ireland, Germany, Chile, Mexico, Hawaii, China, and Australia. Many had engaged in mining in their homelands. The miners were predominantly young and male, with men accounting for more than 90 percent of gold rush migrants to California. They were also incredibly mobile, moving from strike to strike as surface deposits were depleted. This transient, male-dominated, and ethnically diverse climate of the early mining camps produced a tumultuous and violent society. Miners organized governing structures to oversee mining claims and water rights, but most other disputes were resolved through fists, guns, or vigilantism. Throughout the gold rush years, the vigilantes' victims were disproportionately Chinese, Mexican, and other nonwhite miners who competed with, and were violently expelled by, their Anglo rivals.

In reality, only a small percentage of miners struck it rich—those who were lucky enough to get there first and those who profited by selling goods and services to fellow prospectors. Once the surface deposits had been skimmed off through placer mining (using hand tools such as picks, shovels, and buckets), prospectors fanned out to new strikes along the Feather and Stanislaus rivers in California and, in 1859, a major silver discovery in Nevada called the Comstock Lode. That same year, gold was discovered along Cherry Creek in Colorado, and within a few years prospectors were swarming to gold and silver strikes in Idaho and Montana as well. Those who stayed in California ended up working for newly established companies that could afford the machinery and extensive labor force necessary to tap underground ore deposits through shaft or hydraulic mining. The same cycle ensued in other areas as small-scale placer miners gave way to large mining companies financed with California or eastern capital. The once independent prospector was thus transformed into a wage laborer in a matter of a few years.[17]

Although gold and silver fueled the early hard rock mining booms, the largest western mining corporations developed around copper, coal, and other less precious minerals that were nonetheless vital to the country's industrial development. Used to make electrical wiring, copper was discovered in Montana, Arizona, and Utah, and major mining operations commenced there in the 1880s and 1890s. Copper production, requiring costly smelting and refining, came to be dominated by three corporate giants: Anaconda (financed by the Rockefellers), Kennecott (financed by the Guggenheims), and Phelps Dodge. The Rockefeller family also controlled the western coal industry, including the mammoth Colorado Fuel and Iron Company, which operated thirty-eight facilities and employed thirteen thousand workers in Colorado and other western states in 1900.[18] The extensive resources of the coal and copper mining regions and the vast labor required to extract them attracted thousands of migrant workers to these areas. To head off labor organizing, coal and copper mine owners built company-run towns in which they owned and operated all housing, schools, businesses, and even churches. In the process, they recouped workers' wages through inflated rents and commodity prices while prohibiting the formation of unions and oppositional political groups.

The large-scale mining operations were labor-intensive and drew on the growing numbers of unskilled immigrant workers entering the United States in the late nineteenth and early twentieth centuries. Earlier generations of skilled Cornish, Irish, and German miners were increasingly joined by unskilled newcomers from Italy, Greece, Mexico, and the Balkans. The newer immigrants were concentrated in unskilled, lower-paying jobs: loading and pushing cars, removing rubble, and working in the mills and smelters. Later, as machine drills and other machinery were introduced, immigrants were employed throughout the industry and came to dominate the population of most western mining towns. They lived in ethnically segregated shack towns or company housing, where living conditions were cramped, primitive, and unsanitary.

The rigid ethnic hierarchy and segregation, however, did not preclude social tensions and violence. In Rock Springs, Wyoming, in 1885, for example, white coal miners employed by the Union Pacific railroad rioted against Chinese workers, a group that the company had initially brought in as strikebreakers in the 1870s. Anti-Chinese sentiment grew over the years as the company gradually replaced white immigrant workers with lower-paid Chinese. Following a dispute over work assignments, the rioters killed twenty-eight Chinese and burned down their camp. The Rock Springs massacre was just one instance in which employers manipulated ethnic animosities to keep workers divided. Racial tensions in mining and other industries resulted in anti-Chinese riots in at least half a dozen western cities in the 1870s and 1880s.[19]

Working conditions in the mines were horrendous. Many who worked underground labored for ten hours a day, often in temperatures of a hundred degrees or more. Lacking proper ventilation, the shafts were plagued by high levels of dust and carbon dioxide and wreaked of fumes from blasting powder, sweat, and human waste. More critically, accidents caused by explosions, fires, floods, cave-ins, and machinery mishaps made mining one of the world's most dangerous occupations. In the 1870s, one out of thirty miners in the Comstock Lode was permanently disabled each year, while one out of eighty was killed. Those who survived still ran a substantial risk of developing respiratory disease. In Butte, Montana, nearly half of all miners sampled during World War I had contracted tuberculosis or silicosis. For those who spent a lifetime working in the mines, the possibility of death, disease, or disablement was very real.[20]

Understandably, mine workers sought to protect their occupational interests. Beginning in the Comstock Lode in the 1860s, hard rock miners organized mutual aid societies to provide injury and death benefits to miners and their families. They also organized unions to protest the wage cuts that mine owners repeatedly instituted, and like other workers of the period, they demanded an eight-hour day. By the 1870s, miners' unions were established in most of the West's major hard rock mining camps. These local unions scored many successes in the boom years of the 1870s and early 1880s, and places such as Virginia City, Nevada, and Butte, Montana, became bulwarks of union power. A sharp decline in silver prices in the mid-eighties, however, resulted in widespread wage cuts and unsuccessful strikes that weakened the movement. Metal prices plunged further during the financial panic of 1893, depressing the entire western mining industry. Mine owners slashed wages or shut down, and some began to break up the unions by hiring spies to infiltrate them, firing union workers, and using violence to drive labor organizers out of the camps.

One of the fiercest battles occurred in the Coeur d'Alene mining region of northern Idaho in 1892. Founded in 1891, the Coeur d'Alene Miners' Union fought to maintain a minimum wage of $3.50 per day. In response, employers organized the Mine Owners' Protective Association (MOA) and vowed to break the union. They hired Pinkerton detectives to infiltrate the union, locked workers out for several months, and then reopened with substantial wage cuts. When the union called a strike, the MOA imported strikebreakers under armed guard and secured federal injunctions against union interference with mine operations. Frustrated strikers took up arms and stormed the mines, ejecting the scabs and company guards. Several men were killed in these clashes, and the Frisco Mill was destroyed when a group of miners set off dynamite. With threats of further violence against company property, the MOA convinced the governor to declare martial law, and the state and federal governments dispatched troops. Before long, company guards backed by the troops arrested more than three hundred union members and sympathizers, herding them into makeshift prison camps known as bullpens, where they languished for weeks. Most of the union's officers were later imprisoned on conspiracy charges, and the strike was broken.[21]

The bitter outcome at Coeur d'Alene convinced union leaders that they needed a stronger, more united movement across the western states. The next year, union leaders meeting in Butte formed the Western Federation of Miners (WFM), a militant union committed to representing all mine workers regardless of skill—an approach known as industrial unionism. Under the leadership of William "Big Bill" Haywood, the WFM came to encompass two hundred local unions representing some fifty thousand members. The federation provided support for striking locals and hired organizers to bring in new members. It also embraced an avowedly socialist agenda and established hospitals and mutual aid networks in dozens of mining communities. Some of its leaders helped found the radical Industrial Workers of the World in 1905, while others called on workers to take up arms against intransigent employers. From 1893 through World War I, the WFM and other mining unions clashed with employers in an escalating cycle of strikes and violence.

Colorado proved to be the epicenter of this mining-related violence. During the depression years of the 1890s, the WFM set out to organize the state's metal miners as employers cut wages and increased working hours. Violent strikes ensued at Cripple Creek in 1894, Leadville in 1896, and Telluride in 1901 and 1903–1904. Mine owners in all three areas appealed to the governor to send in the militia, effectively breaking the strikes in Leadville and Telluride. The biggest conflict, however, occurred in Cripple Creek in 1903–1904, when the WFM struck over the company's refusal to allow union organizing among lower-paid mill and smelter workers. The strike continued for months and was punctuated by violence, including an explosion set off by a union sympathizer that destroyed a railroad station and killed thirteen strikebreakers. Once again, employers appealed to the governor to send in the state militia but also organized the Citizens Alliance, an anti-union vigilante group comprising local merchants and businessmen. Such middle-class townspeople had provided critical support to miners in earlier strikes, but popular violence directed at unions and their business supporters eventually eroded those bonds. With the help of the troops, the Citizens Alliance rounded up 238 union leaders and strikers at gunpoint and forcibly expelled them from the state. The strike was broken by the end of the year, and the company replaced most of the union workers with unorganized immigrant workers from eastern and southern Europe.[22]

THE COLORADO COAL STRIKE

Although labor conflict was most evident in the state's hard rock mines, trouble was also brewing in the soft coal mining areas of southern Colorado. The state contained some of the nation's largest bituminous coal reserves, and companies had been extracting coal there since the construction of railroad lines in the 1870s. While there were substantial deposits in the state's northern region, the largest and most accessible coalfields lay just east of the Sangre de Cristo Mountains in the southern counties of Las Animas and Huerfano. Springing up along the Purgatory River, the mining towns of Walsenburg, Ludlow, and Trinidad quickly became home to thousands of incoming miners. Among the many companies working the southern fields, Colorado Fuel and Iron (CFI) was the largest. In 1902, John D. Rockefeller Sr. bought a controlling interest in CFI and set out to increase its profitability by making stronger efforts to ensure a nonunion labor force.

CFI's chief rival was the United Mine Workers of America (UMWA), a union founded in 1890 by workers in the anthracite coal mines of Ohio, Pennsylvania, and other states east of the Mississippi. Representing 200,000 mostly eastern miners, the UMWA steered a conservative course in the 1890s and showed little interest in expanding into the vast unorganized coalfields of the West. But the militancy of the Western Federation of Miners was infectious, and grassroots efforts to organize UMWA locals in Colorado were soon under way. With only a small membership base in 1894, the UMWA failed in its initial strike. In 1903, however, the growing UMWA locals led a walkout of nearly 10,000 Colorado coal miners demanding increased wages and an eight-hour day.

Determined to thwart the expanding union movement, CFI and other coal operators followed the example of the state's hard rock employers by hiring detectives and armed guards, importing strikebreakers, and then appealing for a declaration of martial law. In the meantime, coal operators in the northern counties settled with the UMWA, thus sundering a regional organizing effort and leaving the southern miners to fight alone. In early 1904, Governor James Peabody complied with employers' requests and dispatched troops to the southern strike zone. During their ten-week deployment, troops worked with the local Citizens Alliance to arrest 164 union leaders and sympathizers, 100 of whom were forcibly expelled from the state. Among them was Mary Harris "Mother" Jones, a fiery elderly UMWA speaker and itinerant organizer who had come to Trinidad to rally the flagging spirits of the strikers. The mass arrests and expulsions crippled the strike effort, which eventually collapsed that summer.[23]

In the wake of the union's defeat, CFI and other employers replaced the formerly union-friendly workforce with unorganized workers from Italy, Austria, Poland, Serbia, Croatia, and Montenegro. Within a few years, large numbers of Greek and Mexican immigrants would join them. By 1910, more than 70 percent of the coal miners in Las Animas and Huerfano counties were foreign-born and non-English-speaking, and more than twenty different languages were spoken there. As in other western mining communities, the influx of new immigrants marked a major ethnic transformation in the workforce. The resulting ethnic tensions and language barriers made unionization more difficult.

Although the composition of the workforce shifted dramatically, wages, working hours, and working conditions remained unchanged. Unlike metal miners, who typically earned from three to four dollars a day, coal miners were paid by weight for the coal they dug. Any other necessary work, such as timbering (building structural supports), clearing coal car tracks, washing the coal, and removing impurities, was considered "dead work" and was unpaid. Although miners were required to perform this dead work, the time spent on it ultimately reduced their wages. They were thus effectively encouraged to skimp on timbering and other safety measures. Miners were also subject to underweighing by company weight checkers, whose scales were sometimes found to be several hundred pounds light. Moreover, coal miners worked long and irregular hours, putting in ten- to twelve-hour days in the rush season. Long layoffs, however, meant that most coal miners worked fewer than two hundred days a year. The Colorado Bureau of Labor Statistics estimated that in 1912 miners netted an average of only $1.68 per day, out of which they had to pay rent for company-owned houses. They were also compelled to buy goods in company stores with profit margins of 20 percent or more. Not surprisingly, miners consistently pushed for increased wages and an eight-hour day, with little success.[24]

Hazardous working conditions were an even greater concern. For years, the UMWA had pressed for mine safety laws, but those that were passed were rarely enforced. When rare visits from state mine inspectors occurred, employers usually got advance notice. One of the most critical problems was the buildup of coal dust in the mines, which generated highly flammable gases that were a frequent cause of explosions. Mine operators were required by state law to water down the dust regularly, but arid conditions and distant water sources made the practice costly and difficult. The result was a string of mining disasters: twenty-four workers killed at the Primero Mine in January 1907; seventy-five fatalities in another explosion at the same mine in January 1910; fifty-six lives lost at the Starkville Mine in October 1910; and eighty-two deaths at the Delagua Mine four weeks later. The mining companies denied responsibility for the accidents, blaming them on workers' carelessness. These recurring disasters gave Colorado miners the highest death rate in the country.

Horrific mine accidents coupled with a change in UMWA leadership helped rekindle union activism in Colorado. Led by John Lawson, a fearless organizer and veteran of the 1903–1904 strike, the UMWA launched a successful organizing campaign in the northern coalfields in 1908. But in the more repressive southern counties of Las Animas and Huerfano, the UMWA ran into formidable resistance. Working undercover, UMWA organizers had to sneak into mining camps at night or meet with sympathetic workers around campfires in the mountains. When caught (often with the help of company detectives), organizers were arrested, beaten, and run out of town. After five years of unsuccessful stealth organizing, the national leadership of the UMWA launched a full-scale unionization campaign in July 1913 and dispatched forty-two organizers to the Trinidad coalfield.

To root out unionization efforts, employers hired hundreds of armed mine guards and detectives from the Baldwin-Felts Agency. Tensions between detectives and union organizers dated back to earlier mining struggles in Pennsylvania, Ohio, and Kentucky, and hostilities between the two quickly escalated. On August 16, an Italian American organizer named Gerald Lippiatt was fatally shot by two Baldwin-Felts detectives in downtown Trinidad following a heated exchange. A coroner's jury declared the killing to be justifiable homicide, which outraged labor supporters. Workers' anger over Lippiatt's killing accelerated local organizing efforts, and on September 16, union delegates meeting in Trinidad voted to strike the following week.

The coal companies immediately evicted striking workers from their company-owned houses, leaving some eleven thousand workers homeless. Within days, the union set up tent camps in Ludlow, Aguilar, Forbes, Sopris, Segundo, and Walsenburg. The Ludlow camp was the largest, housing more than a thousand men, women, and children who spoke twenty-two different languages. Violence broke out almost immediately as UMWA strikers and their families clashed with mine guards and strikebreakers. Over the next month, at least nine men were killed in these conflicts, including one striker at the Forbes tent camp on October 17, four strikers in Walsenburg on October 24, and one mine guard near the Primero mine on October 25.

To quell the disorder, the coal operators convinced Governor Elias Ammons to declare martial law and send in the Colorado National Guard. On October 29, two cavalry troops, two infantry regiments, and a field artillery detachment entered the strike zone under the command of General John Chase. Although the strikers initially welcomed the troops as protectors, relations quickly soured, with strikers killing three mine guards and a strikebreaker on November 8. Hostilities intensified, particularly between strikers and members of Company B, a unit led by Lieutenant Karl Linderfelt that included many former mine guards. As regular troops returned home over the winter, a growing number of mine guards and coal company employees took their places, while the coal operators provided pay, vehicles, and other equipment to the militia. In late November, National Guard troops began escorting workers into the mines after Governor Ammons rescinded his earlier order barring strikebreakers from the area. Over the next few months, strikers complained of abusive treatment by soldiers, illegal searches and arrests, unlawful detentions, prisoner abuse, and other violations of civil rights. The arrest of Louis Tikas and other UMWA organizers in December was particularly galling to labor supporters.

Women joined protests and other strike-related activities, including a march of strikers' wives and children on January 22, 1914, that resulted in a violent clash with National Guard troops. The women's activism was partly inspired by Mother Jones, who was imprisoned in a local hospital. An Irish-born daughter of a working-class family, Mother Jones had lost her husband and family to a yellow fever epidemic many years earlier and now worked as an itinerant labor organizer. She was invited to address the miners in Trinidad in September 1913, and her fiery speech helped launch the Colorado strike. In the months that followed, her presence in the strike zone galvanized activism among strikers and their wives, leading to her repeated arrest and removal from the area. This harsh treatment of a seventy-six-year-old woman[25] reflected poorly on the employers and state authorities who sanctioned it.

Plagued by controversy and fiscal burdens, Governor Ammons withdrew most of the National Guard troops that spring. By mid-April 1914, only thirty-five soldiers of the notorious Company B remained. On April 18, another one hundred men—mainly managers, office workers, and mine guards on the payroll of the local coal companies—were formed into an additional company.

Two days later, on April 20, a sudden outbreak of violence, sparked by gunfire from an unknown source, resulted in mass bloodshed at the Ludlow tent colony. Besieged miners fled to the hills with their rifles and engaged in a daylong firefight with the heavily armed militia. That evening, dozens of women and children escaped from the camp and fled to surrounding ranches as the tents caught fire. By the next day, the Ludlow camp had burned to the ground and twenty people lay dead, including two women and eleven children whose bodies were recovered from a pit beneath one of the tents (Figure 2). The incident was one of the most tragic episodes in American labor history.

(opposite) **Figure 2.** *The Aftermath in Ludlow, 1914*

An onlooker surveys the burnt remains of the Ludlow tent colony following the April 20, 1914, clash that left twenty people dead, including thirteen women and children.

Near View Of Ruins
Ludlow Tent Colony

In the days that followed, miners and their families gathered in Trinidad to pay their respects at a series of mass funerals. As families shared their grief and called for redress, the miners vowed to take up arms and continue the fight. On April 22, UMWA leaders issued a "call to arms" urging union men "to protect the workers of Colorado against the murder and cremation of men, women, and children by armed assassins in the employ of the coal corporations, serving under the guise of state militiamen." Hundreds of men took to the hills, where armed supporters from around the state joined them. Over the next week, the rebels set fire to six tipples and dynamited several mines, causing millions of dollars in damage. At least thirty more people, mainly mine guards and strikebreakers, died.

Public outrage over the Ludlow Massacre, as it came to be called, was widespread, with mass protests in Denver, New York, Chicago, and San Francisco. As protests flared and the violence in Colorado continued, Governor Ammons appealed to President Woodrow Wilson to send federal troops. On April 28, Wilson ordered the U.S. Army into Colorado, deploying more than sixteen hundred troops that brought an end to the fighting. The strike dragged on for another seven months, however, and the coal companies gradually resumed operations using nonunion labor protected by U.S. troops. Later attempts at federal mediation failed when coal operators refused a proposed settlement. On December 10, 1914, the UMWA admitted defeat and called off the strike.

All told, at least seventy-five people died in strike-related violence in Colorado in 1913–1914. More than four hundred strikers were indicted on charges of murder and other crimes, including UMWA leader John Lawson, who was convicted of killing a mine guard and sentenced to life in prison. Lawson's conviction was later overturned, as were the other convictions. On the opposing side, no mine guards or company managers were ever tried for strike-related violence, and the National Guard troops and officers who faced courts-martial were all exonerated. Nevertheless, the Ludlow Massacre had sent shock waves around the country.

Indeed, the magnitude of the Ludlow tragedy stirred extensive public debate over labor and industrial conditions. In 1914–1915, the U.S. Commission on Industrial Relations conducted a major investigation of the Colorado strike and Ludlow killings and issued a lengthy report (Documents 18, 19, 26, and 27). Ultimately, its pro-labor recommendations were largely ignored. Nevertheless, the negative publicity surrounding Ludlow badly tarnished the reputations of Rockefeller and

CFI. Determined to repair his image, Rockefeller embarked on a two-pronged campaign of public relations and industrial reform. He hired a public relations expert, who devised a series of pamphlets about the strike, casting the miners' union as a corrupt culprit in the violence. In 1915, Rockefeller launched the Colorado Industrial Representation Plan. Designed to foster harmony between labor and capital, the plan became an influential model for scores of company-sponsored unions and industrial reforms in the 1920s.

THE TAMING OF THE WEST

Mining towns were not the only sites of labor unrest in the West. During the 1910s, the Industrial Workers of the World (IWW), or Wobblies, took up organizing campaigns among itinerant agricultural and timber workers in California and the Pacific Northwest. Founded by WFM radicals in 1905, the IWW was a militant, anticapitalist union that stressed the solidarity of all workers regardless of skill, race, or gender. While prevalent in textile mills in the Northeast, the Wobblies were particularly strong among the migrant workers of the West, who faced brutal living and working conditions in remote camps and mills. Meeting bitter resistance from employers, the IWW launched a wave of "free speech" fights in more than twenty western towns, where it attempted to expose the exploitation of workers. In several locations, employers and conservatives opposed to the Wobblies' revolutionary ideology used violence and intimidation to silence the free speech movement. Some of the worst violence occurred in Everett, Washington, in 1916, where armed vigilantes attacked Wobblies trying to organize local mill workers, killing at least seven and injuring dozens more.

U.S. involvement in World War I served to heighten anti-immigrant and antiradical sentiment, and patriotic groups branded the IWW (which opposed the war) as a treasonous organization. This wartime sentiment helped stir violence against IWW strikers in Bisbee, Arizona, in 1917. When Mexican and other immigrant mine workers struck for higher wages that summer, local posses rounded up nearly twelve hundred strikers, loaded them onto train cars, and transported them to the New Mexico desert, abandoning them without shelter, food, or water. Two years later, in 1919, members of the American Legion in Centralia, Washington, attacked local Wobblies as part of a patriotic event celebrating the end of the war. Five people were killed. Following the war, the ensuing Red Scare effectively destroyed the organization.

In many ways, however, World War I was the last gasp of the West's violent wars of incorporation. After the war, the number of mining and range wars diminished as frontier outposts gave way to settled communities and as corporate reforms, labor unions, expanded local law enforcement, and federal regulatory agencies mitigated violent social conflict. Moreover, by the 1920s the incorporation of the West into a national industrial market was largely complete. In many areas, wealthy organized interests had successfully consolidated their control of western lands and resources and become dominant forces in politics. In other places, the depletion of resources caused larger operators to leave, ceding control to smaller, local enterprises. In some ranching areas, large cattle operators eventually closed down as poor grazing conditions undercut their profits. In their wake, a more frugal group of family-run farmer-ranchers emerged, who raised winter feed to support smaller herds of cattle or sheep. This system reduced winter grazing on the public ranges and eliminated the maverick problem. In the mining districts, some of the most violent camps became ghost towns as ore deposits were exhausted. Others, particularly in copper and coal mining areas, became permanent towns with schools, churches, unions, and civic organizations that helped promote social order.

Beginning in the Progressive Era and especially in the 1930s, the federal government became a major player in western land and labor affairs. The rise of national conservation agencies such as the U.S. Forest Service (founded in 1905) and the U.S. Grazing Service (established in 1934 and succeeded by the Bureau of Land Management in 1946) established a system of grazing permits for federal rangelands to regulate land use. Certainly, disputes over rangelands have continued into the twenty-first century, and large ranchers have wielded heavy influence over government policymaking. But these conflicts have been mostly fought by lawyers with pens rather than cowboys with six-guns.

In the 1930s, the U.S. government helped shape labor relations in the West by providing employment to thousands of workers building dams, irrigation systems, and other federal projects initiated under the New Deal. During the hardships of the Great Depression, federal agencies constructed model labor camps for farmworkers and dispensed relief funds to the unemployed. Finally, with the passage of the National Labor Relations Act in 1935, the federal government guaranteed labor's right to organize, spurring major unionization campaigns in the West and nationwide. Western miners, mill workers, agricultural laborers, and longshoremen heeded the call, organizing unions under the Congress of Industrial Organizations (CIO). While there had been a surge of violent strikes in the early 1930s, the federally sanctioned organizing campaigns of the late 1930s and 1940s were largely non-violent.

FBI crime statistics confirm that the West was notably less violent after 1930, with homicide rates in most western states lower than in the nation as a whole. This trend continued until the 1960s, when violent crime rates in the West spiked upward, as they did in the country generally. Despite high rates of violent crime in heavily urbanized states such as California, Texas, and Nevada, most western states today continue to post homicide rates far below the national average. Western violence, for the most part, was a product of the frontier era and has not been a significant factor in the region's history for many decades.

Although the frontier conditions that fueled western violence are long gone, the values, images, and symbols of the Wild West live on in our collective memory and culture. The staged shoot-outs in Deadwood, South Dakota, and Tombstone, Arizona, are just one example of the ongoing fascination with western violence, as are hundreds of popular western films, songs, and novels. Our heritage of western violence also has a political dimension. Presidents from Theodore Roosevelt to George W. Bush have adorned the White House with western artworks depicting cowboys, Indians, and cavalrymen. And that most popular of western movie actors, John Wayne, was a favorite of President Ronald Reagan. It is not surprising, then, that recent presidents (many of whom are from the South or West) have used cowboy language and imagery to justify wars from Vietnam to Iraq. But not all western violence has become part of our collective memory. Some horrific incidents of racial and class conflict, such as the Ludlow Massacre, have been all but forgotten. These episodes are equally important, however, if we are to understand the legacy of frontier violence in contemporary American life.

NOTES

[1]Richard Slotkin, *The Fatal Environment: The Myth of the Frontier in the Age of Industrialization, 1800–1890* (New York: Atheneum, 1985).

[2]Russell Thornton, *American Indian Holocaust and Survival* (Norman: University of Oklahoma Press, 1987), 133.

[3]Clare V. McKanna, *Homicide, Race, and Justice in the American West, 1880–1920* (Tucson: University of Arizona Press, 1997); Roger McGrath, *Gunfighters, Highwaymen, and Vigilantes: Violence on the Frontier* (Berkeley: University of California Press, 1984). As some historians note, even these homicide figures must be viewed skeptically, as they come mainly from frontier towns whose small populations can produce artificially inflated rates of homicide when calculated per 100,000. But a recent study of San Francisco, a much larger community, also reveals high rates of homicide in the nineteenth century compared to eastern cities. See Robert R. Dykstra, "Violence, Gender, and Methodology in the 'New' Western History," *Reviews in American History* 27 (March 1999): 79–86; Kevin Mullen, *Dangerous Strangers: Minority Newcomers and Criminal Violence in San Francisco, 1850–2000* (New York: Palgrave-Macmillan, 2005), 4, 85.

[4]Richard Maxwell Brown, *No Duty to Retreat: Violence and Values in American History and Society* (New York: Oxford University Press, 1991).

[5]McGrath, *Gunfighters, Highwaymen, and Vigilantes*, 247–51.

[6]For a gender analysis of western violence, see David T. Courtwright, *Violent Land: Single Men and Social Disorder from the Frontier to the Inner City* (Cambridge, Mass.: Harvard University Press, 1996).

[7]Linda Gordon, *The Great Arizona Orphan Abduction* (Cambridge, Mass.: Harvard University Press, 1999).

[8]Richard Maxwell Brown, *Strain of Violence: Historical Studies of American Violence and Vigilantism* (New York: Oxford University Press, 1975), chap. 4. Brown's data defines vigilante movements as organized extralegal groups that operated for a period of time (usually months or weeks) and generally undertook multiple actions. It does not, therefore, include most lynchings in the South, which were more spontaneous killings. The Ku Klux Klan and other white supremacist groups, however, would seem to fit this definition of vigilantism. With hundreds of Klan killings during Reconstruction alone, it is fair to say that the South, along with the West, was a major center of vigilantism in this period.

[9]Ibid.

[10]Richard Maxwell Brown, "Violence," in *The Oxford History of the American West*, ed. Clyde Milner, Carol O'Connor, and Martha A. Sandweiss, 393–425 (New York: Oxford University Press, 1994).

[11]Ibid.

[12]Robert R. Dykstra, *The Cattle Towns* (New York: Knopf, 1968).

[13]Richard White, "Animals and Enterprise," in *The Oxford History of the American West*, ed. Clyde Milner, Carol O'Connor, and Martha A. Sandweiss, 237–73 (New York: Oxford University Press, 1994).

[14]Harry Sinclair Drago, *The Great Range Wars: Violence on the Grasslands* (Lincoln: University of Nebraska Press, 1970).

[15]An earlier group, the Laramie County Stock Association, was founded in 1872 in southeastern Wyoming. It changed its name to the Wyoming Stock Growers Association in 1879 to reflect its now territory-wide membership.

[16]Frank N. Schubert, "The Suggs Affray: The Black Cavalry in the Johnson County War," *Western Historical Quarterly* 4 (January 1973): 60.

[17]For a good summary of the industrialization of western mining, see Patricia Nelson Limerick, *The Legacy of Conquest: The Unbroken Past of the American West* (New York: Norton, 1988), chap. 4.

[18]Carlos Schwantes, "Wage Earners and Wealth Makers," *The Oxford History of the American West*, ed. Clyde Milner, Carol O'Connor, and Martha A. Sandweiss, 433–34 (New York: Oxford University Press, 1994).

[19]Craig Storti, *Incident at Bitter Creek: The Story of the Rock Springs Chinese Massacre* (Ames: Iowa State University Press, 1991).

[20]Richard White, *"It's Your Misfortune and None of My Own": A New History of the American West* (Norman: University of Oklahoma Press, 1991), 281.

[21]Richard E. Lingenfelter, *The Hardrock Miners: A History of the Mining Labor Movement in the West, 1863–1893* (Berkeley: University of California Press, 1974), 196–218.

[22]Elizabeth Jameson, *All That Glitters: Class, Conflict, and Community in Cripple Creek* (Urbana: University of Illinois Press, 1998).

[23]George McGovern and Leonard Guttridge, *The Great Coalfield War* (Boston: Houghton Mifflin, 1972), chap. 3.

[24]Ibid., 20–22.

[25]Mother Jones claimed to be born in 1830, but biographer Elliott Gorn's research indicates that she was actually born in 1837. She thus embellished her image as a "white-haired" motherly organizer manhandled by authorities. Elliott J. Gorn, *Mother Jones: The Most Dangerous Woman in America* (New York: Hill & Wang, 2001), 57.

The Documents

PART TWO

The Documents

1

The Johnson County War

1

WALTER BARON VON RICHTHOFEN

Cattle Raising on the Plains of North America
1885

Beginning in Texas in the 1860s, the cattle boom spread northward to Colorado, Wyoming, Nebraska, and Montana over the next two decades. A spate of articles and books celebrating the West's boundless opportunities encouraged this expansion. Among them was Walter Baron Von Richthofen's Cattle Raising on the Plains of North America, *published in 1885. A Prussian baron who immigrated to the United States, Von Richthofen settled in Denver in the late 1870s. There he ran a horse and dairy farm and invested in real estate. Although there is no evidence that he ever owned cattle, his glowing reports of western ranching and its potential profits helped fuel the cattle bonanza of the 1880s.*

Profits in Cattle-Raising, and Fortunes Made Therein

The immense profits which have been universally realized in the Western cattle business for the past, and which will be increased in the future, owing to the more economical methods pursued, so long as ranges can be purchased at present prices, may seem incredible to many of my readers, who, no doubt, have considered the stories of the

From Walter Baron Von Richthofen, *Cattle Raising on the Plains of North America* (1885; repr., Norman: University of Oklahoma Press, 1964), 70–73, 80.

fortunes realized as myths. Yet it is true that many men who started only a few years ago with comparatively few cattle, are now wealthy, and, in some cases, millionaires. They certainly did not find the gold upon the prairies, nor did they have any source of revenue beyond the increase of their cattle. The agencies producing this immense wealth are very natural and apparent.

The climate of the West is the healthiest on the earth; the pure, high mountain air and dry atmosphere are the natural remedies, or rather preventives, against sickness among cattle in general, and against all epidemic diseases in particular; for "nowhere in the Western states do we find any traces of pleuro-pneumonia, foot or mouth, and such like contagious diseases."

The pure, clear water of the mountain rivers affords to cattle another health preserver, and the fine nutritious and bountiful grasses, and in winter the naturally cured hay, furnish to them the healthiest natural food.

Formerly these pastures cost nothing, and at present only a trifle, . . . so that the interest on the investment in purchasing land is of little importance in the estimate of the cost of keeping a herd. In fact, ownership of land is now indispensable for a herd-owner. This land in less than ten years will be a considerable factor in the profits of the cattle business, as the value of pastures will constantly increase.

The principal cost of raising cattle is only the herding and watching the cattle by herders, without any cost for sheltering or feeding. In time even these expenses will be reduced, as now already herds are kept in large fenced ranges, and many of the herders are dispensed with.

The losses of cattle, as shown by statistics, are larger among Eastern and European herds, which are sheltered in stables and fed the whole year round, than among the shelterless herds of the West.

The losses in the West . . . are practically reduced by long experience to a certain percentage, which enables the stockmen to calculate infallibly the profits and losses of their business.

This annual loss is found to average 2 to 3 per cent. We may safely put the loss in the extreme Northern states at about 3 per cent, and in the more Southern and temperate districts at 2 or less per cent.

The annual cost of herding the cattle . . . is about $.70 per head; adding the other expenses, such as taxes, loss of interest on the purchase-money of land, etc., we find that the entire annual expense is less than $1.50 per head.

It takes a heifer calf, say, three years to mature, and a steer calf will be ready for the market in four years. The latter will then bring $40.00; deducting the $6.00 of expense for his rearing, we have a net profit of $34.00 on each steer.

Now let me illustrate the profits realized from one Texas cow, worth $30.00. In ten years she will have eight calves, which, if they are all steers, will have produced at the end of fourteen years $320, or a profit of $272.00. The cow herself still remains, and is worth about her original cost for the butcher. These figures are made without reference to any increase in the value of cattle or beef, and without reference to any improvement of the stock by crossing it with better blood. . . .

The following is a statement of the business of a banker of Denver, who does not wish his name thus advertised:

In 1878 he bought 320 head of cattle for	$ 4,000
In 1879 he bought 1,000 head of cattle for	10,000
In 1880 he bought 1,900 head of cattle for	20,000
In 1882 he bought 1,900 head of cattle for	38,500
	$72,500
Horses and ranch	3,500
Total	$76,000
In 1880 he sold steers for	$ 5,500
In 1881 he sold steers for	13,000
In 1882 he sold steers for	27,500
In 1883 he sold steers for	150,000
Total	$196,000

The net profit of his business in five years was $120,000.

Ten years ago an Irish servant-girl wanted money due her, amounting to $150, from a cattle-raiser who lived in Montana. Cattle had been dull, and he could not dispose of any of his herd, but agreed to her to brand fifteen cows in her name, give her the increase, and carry them with his herd, free of cost, until she was ready to sell, he to have the first privilege of purchase. She accepted, held on to her purchase, and last May sold out to her master for $25,000.

2

EMERSON HOUGH

The Rustler

1897

Emerson Hough was an author and journalist who published more than thirty books and hundreds of newspaper and magazine articles, many of them on the American West. Born in Iowa in 1857, Hough moved to New Mexico Territory in 1883, just as the Lincoln County range wars there were drawing to a close. Working as a reporter for a local paper, Hough also began writing stories for Forest and Stream *and other outdoor sporting magazines that were becoming increasingly popular back east. In 1897, he was invited to write a book about cowboys for a series on the history of the West. The resulting volume,* The Story of the Cowboy, *was published in 1897 to critical acclaim, including an endorsement from fellow western enthusiast Theodore Roosevelt.* The Story of the Cowboy *is still considered a classic document on the history of the cattle industry and includes a thoughtful account of the disputed meaning of* rustling *and the role it played in fueling conflicts such as the Johnson County War.*

There has never been upon the range a character more fully discussed or less fully understood [than that somewhat famous Western character known as the rustler]. Many persons are familiar with the curious Western verb "to rustle," and know what is meant when one is asked to "rustle a little wood" for the camp in the mountains, or when it is announced that the horses should be turned out to "rustle a little grass," etc.; but they would be unable, as indeed perhaps many resident cattle men might be unable, to give the original derivation of the term "rustler."

Any one acquainted with the cattle country of the North would soon come to hear much of the rustler, and that in stories of the most confusing character. Thus he might hear of the murder of some dweller in an

From Emerson Hough, *The Story of the Cowboy* (1897; repr., New York: Appleton, 1912), 272–77.

outlying camp, and be informed that the crime was attributed to "rustlers." A stagecoach might be held up, or a mountain treasure train robbed, and the act would be laid at the door of this same mysterious being, the rustler. He might hear that a number of men had been the victims of a lynching bee, and be advised that the men hung were rustlers. Thus in time he might come to believe that any and all bad characters of the West were to be called rustlers. In this he would be inaccurate and unjust. The real rustler was an operator in a more restricted field, and although it would be impossible to induce a cattle man to believe there was ever any such thing as a good rustler, it is at least true that there were sometimes two sides to the rustler's case. . . . In the later or acquired sense of the term, all rustlers were criminals. In the original sense of the word, no rustler was a criminal. He was simply a hard-working man, paid a little gratuity for a little extra exertion on his part. He got his name in the early Maverick days, before the present strict laws governing the handling of that inviting range product. He was then a cowboy pure and simple, and sometimes his employer gave him two, three, or five dollars for each Maverick he found and branded to the home brand. Then the cattle associations for a time paid any cowboy five dollars a head for any Maverick he found for the association. It behooved the cowboys of those days to "get out and rustle" for calves, the word being something of a synonym for the city slang word "hustle," and with no evil meaning attached to it. The term passed through some years of evolution before it gained its proper modern significance, or the improper and inaccurate use which is sometimes given it.

Under the system of Maverick gratuities the cowboy prospered on the northern range. Those were his palmy days. Any cowpuncher of active habits and a saving disposition could easily lay up considerable sums of money each year. As he was bred upon the range and under-stood nothing but the cow business, it was the most natural thing in the world for him to buy a few cows and start in business for himself, sometimes while still under pay of his former employer, and sometimes quite "on his own hook." He gradually began his herd, and had his brand registered as those of the cowmen of the district. Thus he ceased to be cowboy and became cowman; or rather he remained as he really always was, both cowboy and cowman, both herder and owner. In this way many young men who went on the range "broke" began in a short time to "get ahead" very rapidly. There were few better avenues to quick fortunes than those offered by the cattle busi-ness at this stage of its growth. The logical sequel followed very rapidly. From all parts of the country all sorts of men pressed into the business. There appeared upon the range a great many men of the sort known to the old-time cowmen as "bootblack cowpunchers," men who came from the Eastern country to go into the cattle business for what money there was in it, and who were not slow to see where the quick ways of making money might be made still a little quicker. There also came into the business a great many Eastern men of wealth and standing, who were wise enough to see that the cattle business offered profits fairly Midaslike compared to the possibilities of capital in the older country. The West was now settling up rapidly along all the railroads with a good class of citizens, men of culture and refinement among them, all pressing into the new West to "grow up with the country," and to take advantage of the great opportunities of that promised land.

Under this influx of mixed population and this access of new business methods there appeared a factor never before known on the great cattle ranges—that of competition. Heretofore there had always been enough for all. Now there came the stress of the multitude, and with it the dog in the manger which belongs with the ways of modern business life. By this time there began to be hundreds of new brands upon the range, and the wealthy cattle men saw some of their cowboys building up herds in competition with their own. It always grieves the heart of capital to behold a poorer man begin to make too much money. In time there was inaugurated upon the cow range the good old game of the settlements, of dog-eat-dog, and the big dog began to eat the little one. The big men met and combined against the little ones. They agreed that no more Maverick commissions should be paid, and that the cowpuncher need "rustle" no more calves for himself, but should rustle them for his employer only. Moreover, it was agreed that no cowboy should be allowed to own a brand of his own. . . .

This blow at the welfare of the cowboy had a curious effect. It was intended to stop "rustling," but it increased it a thousandfold. It was intended to protect the herds of the big ranchers, but it came near to ruining them. It was intended to stop an honest business system, and it resulted in establishing a dishonest one. It arrayed the written law against the unwritten law which had in all the past been the governing principle of the free West. It threw down the gauntlet for that inevitable war which must be waged between society and the individual; a conflict which can have but one end. In this case that end meant the destruction of all that free and wild character which had for a glorious generation been the distinguishing trait of a great and heroic country. Let us admit that the rustler—who now began to brand calves where he found them, Maverick or no Maverick—was a sinner against the written law, that he was a criminal, that he was the burglar, the bounds-breaker of the range; but let us not forget that he acted in many ways under the stern upholding of what seemed to him the justice of the old West. . . .

. . . To understand [the rustlers'] actions one must endeavour to comprehend clearly what was really the moral code of that time and that country. This code was utterly different from that of the old communities. Under it the man who branded a few calves for himself as an act of "getting even" with the unjust rules of the large cow outfits and the big Eastern syndicates was not lowered in the least in the esteem of his fellow-men, but, to the contrary, was regarded as a man of spirit, and therefore entitled to the rough Western respect which had no eye for him who submitted to be "imposed upon." In some portions of the upper country, notably in a few counties of Wyoming, the rustlers, or men who took beef cattle or calves not their own, far outnumbered the men opposed to them. They were called thieves and cutthroats and outlaws, and so perhaps they were from one standpoint. From their own standpoint they were not, and there were so many of them that they really made the "sovereign people," which is supposed to be the ultimate court of appeal in this country. They elected all the officers and chose the judges in some counties, and they—the people—ran things to suit themselves. It was of no use for a syndicate man[1] to try to get in one of those courts what he called justice, because he was sure to get what the people called justice, and the two were very different things.

[1]A large stock owner, with capital from the East or the British Isles.

3

FRANK M. CANTON

Frontier Trails

1930

The legendary outlaw and lawman Frank Canton was born Joe Horner in Virginia in 1849 and moved with his family to Texas as a child. Convicted and imprisoned for bank robbery in 1877, he later escaped and fled to Nebraska, where he began raising cattle. In the 1880s, he moved to

From Frank M. Canton, *Frontier Trails: The Autobiography of Frank M. Canton* (Norman: University of Oklahoma Press, 1930), 78–82.

Wyoming and was employed as a detective for the Wyoming Stock Grow-
ers Association (WSGA). Settling on a ranch near Buffalo, Wyoming, he
was elected sheriff of Johnson County in 1882. He left office a few years
later to resume employment with the WSGA and would subsequently lead
the regulator campaign that sparked the Johnson County War. In his auto-
biography (published after his death), Canton whitewashed much of his
criminal past, but in this passage he presents the perspective of the big
cattlemen — his employers — on the rustling problem and how it affected
Johnson County prior to 1892.

There were a number of large cattle ranches in Johnson County, on
Powder River, Crazy Woman Creek, Tongue River, and in the Big Horn
Mountains, owned by Englishmen of note who had invested large for-
tunes in that county and were prominent members of the Wyoming
Stock Association. Morton and Richard Frewen owned the '76 Ranch.
Horace Plunkett, who was made famous during the Irish civil trouble in
England and Ireland, owned the E K Ranch. Stewart Wortly, son-in-law
of Admiral Schley, U.S.N., was interested in the C̲ (bar C) Ranch.
William Haywood, an English writer of note, owned the L7 brand.
Other prominent men, such as John Clay, Jr., and Henry Blair, of
Chicago, United States Senators, Francis E. Warren and J. M. Carey, of
Wyoming, Ex-Governor George Baxter, of Wyoming, and many others
too numerous to mention, were owners of cattle ranches.

Besides these there were hundreds of other honest men who
owned from two hundred and fifty to a thousand head of cattle each.
The large ranch owners did not stay at their ranches themselves,
except through the shipping season, but depended entirely upon their
foremen to look after the business and allowed them to select their
own cowboys. These foremen were paid high salaries, and while they
had nothing to do through the long winter months except to draw
their salaries and keep the ice broken in the water holes so that the
range stock could get water, their wages were never reduced, but
remained the same the year around.

But the mistake of selecting the wrong man for foreman was made in
many cases by the large cattle-owners. There was a class of men who
had drifted into that country who were "would-be cowboys," and many
of them had been driven out of Montana by Granville Stuart and the vigilance committees in 1879, and many others had had to leave Texas for
cattle stealing. Not knowing the record of these men and thinking they
were like the majority of cowboys, loyal and true to their employers,

they secured many of their foremen from this class. These foremen then selected their men from the criminal element of their own caliber, and began starting brands of their own. They would ride the range through the winter months on horses owned by their employers, and when they found a calf following a cow that belonged to the man that was paying them wages, they would brand the calf if it was old enough to wean, separate it from its mother and turn it loose. At other times they would brand the calf, then run the cow off in some canyon, shoot her down, and leave the meat for the gray wolves and coyotes.

Each man carried a small iron rod on his saddle, which he called a "running iron," used in blotching and changing brands. The thief, or rustler as he called himself, which was a picturesque, gentlemanly name for a cattle thief, would always select a brand, which he would record in his own name, that would cover most any brand on the range. He would change the ear mark, and with the use of the running iron, could change the old brand so that you could not tell what the original brand was, except in one way, and that was to kill the animal, take the hide off, and look at the inside of the hide which would show a white welt, or scar, so plainly that you could easily tell what the original brand was. The new brand would not show on the inside of the hide. I secured evidence in this way at one time in Montana and convicted three cattle thieves.

The conditions in Johnson County grew from bad to worse. The ranch owners discharged their foremen who had "double-crossed" them, and they also fired a great many of their men. The Stock Association "blackballed" the whole bunch and signed an agreement not to allow any of them to work with the outfit of any member of the Association. The rustlers then banded together and worked the range with pack outfits, in defiance of the laws of the territory and the rules of range work among honest men. There were many honest foremen of cow ranches in that country, such men as Fred Hess, foreman of the '76 Ranch, Frank Laberteaux of the Hoe Ranch, Billie Irvine and Charley Ford of the T A Ranch, Jim Craig, and many others, who stood for law and order and had fought the cattle and horse thieves from the beginning. They also had cowboys of the old school under them whom they could count on under any and all circumstances, but the lawless element had gotten such a start that the officers of the county appeared to be absolutely unable to check them.

In 1888 E. U. Snider retired from the sheriff's office and W. H. Angus, commonly called Red Angus, was elected sheriff. I again accepted a position with the Wyoming Stock Association as range inspector with a commission as Deputy United States Marshal. In a short time I had secured positive evidence in many cases for cattle stealing. The thieves were arrested and brought into court, but it was almost impossible to convict a rustler. The jury was summoned from the body of citizens of the county and friends and sympathizers of the thieves would always manage to get on the jury and turn the defendants loose as fast as we arrested them.

Judge Saufley of Kentucky, who was District Judge at that time, in the trial of a case of six men for cattle stealing who were acquitted, reprimanded the jury in open court and told them that they ought to be prosecuted themselves for turning those men loose. He said that they were the most guilty bunch that ever walked out of a courtroom. It finally got to the point where the honest citizens were afraid to testify against a rustler for fear that their stock would all be stolen and probably their homes burned.

The change in the sheriff's office did not improve the situation so far as making convictions in cattle-stealing cases was concerned. The rustlers got such a foothold that the trial was invariably a farce.

This state of affairs lasted for several years, growing worse all the time. Red Angus was elected sheriff in 1890. There were many common cowpunchers in the rustlers' band who in early days were glad to get a job of "wrangling horses" at twenty-five dollars per month, who now claimed from two hundred and fifty to five hundred cattle each on the range.

4

OSCAR "JACK" FLAGG

The Waterloo of the Barons

1892

Oscar "Jack" Flagg was one of the alleged rustlers targeted by the regulators. Born in West Virginia in 1861, Flagg moved to Texas and began working as a cowboy. He helped his employer move some herds north to Wyoming in 1882 and then settled in Johnson County, where he worked

---

From Oscar H. Flagg, *A Review of the Cattle Business in Johnson County, Wyoming, since 1892 and the Causes That Led to the Recent Invasion* (1892; repr., New York: Arno Press, 1969), 14–17.

for several large cattle outfits. In 1886, Flagg filed for a homestead in the Powder River basin and bought a dozen head of cattle and the "Hat" brand (a registered Wyoming brand purchased from another rancher). Soon after, large cattle owners in the area accused him of branding their mavericks and blackballed him from the Wyoming Stock Growers Association. Flagg became an outspoken critic of the large stock owners, who in turn claimed he was one of the ringleaders of the rustlers. In 1892, Flagg took over the editorship of the Buffalo Bulletin, *the chief newspaper in Johnson County, and published a series of articles presenting his version of events.*

The Winter of 1885 and 1886 passed, and April, 1886, once more found the barons congregated at Cheyenne. Some of them had evidently begun to lose a little of their faith in the country. Instead of being so eager to buy, they now wanted to sell, and during the winter some of them had induced parties who knew nothing of the condition of affairs to buy.

Many a young fellow has cause to regret that he ever met these oily tongued gentlemen, who, with their smooth talk made them think Wyoming was a paradise, and induced them to put their money into their stock companies.

The Peters & Alston Co. sold several thousand calves to two young fellows from Pennsylvania, and the O Bar O outfit sold several thousand head; the price paid being $13 per head. Several other outfits sold calves for the same price.

Although they were selling calves to these tenderfeet they would not sell a one to a cowboy or a poor man in the country.

The summer of 1886 was another dry one, and the calf crop was still smaller than that of the preceding summer. The price of beef was steadily on the decline, the range surely playing out, and the prospect[s] looked very dark.

Expenses were curtailed in every way, the working force was curtailed in every way, the working force was cut down to one-half, and placards having the words in large letters, "Road Ranch, Meals 50 Cents" on them were put up in conspicuous places at nearly all of the ranches and boys out of employment were given to understand that they were not welcome to spend their winters at the cow ranches.[1]

---

[1]A road ranch was a rural restaurant serving cowboys and travelers. Most served liquor, while some also provided lodging and prostitution.

During the last two years a good many homesteads had been taken up by settlers, and some of the boys who had been working for the different outfits had filed on government land. Parties moving in from Nebraska and other states brought small bunches of stock with them; herds driving in from Texas would sell and trade lame and played out cattle, till finally a good many small bunches were owned by the settlers.

All these movements were looked upon as impositions by the "barons." They knew that a maverick was public property and that any man who owned cattle had a right to them. At the stock meeting in the spring of '86 wages were reduced from $40 to $35 per month, and as soon as the round-up started a strike was organized. All work was stopped and word sent to the different managers that no work would go on until they agreed to pay the former wages. They were caught at a disadvantage, work had to be shoved forward, they were obliged to brand their calves and gather beef, and as they had no time to get more men, were obliged to comply with the demands of the strikers and restore their wages. It was done under protest, and as soon as they could get men to fill their places the strikers were either fired or compelled to have their own wages reduced. That summer witnessed the last big round-up in Johnson county. It was not so large as those of former years, but much larger than any one held since.

The winter that was to prove the Waterloo of the barons was approaching. The storms that were to sound their financial death knell and sweep from the plains of Wyoming the source of their wealth, were already gathering in the north. The grass, owing to the country having been overstocked for a number of years was entirely gone, and hardly a vestige of anything on which stock could subsist remained. By the middle of October winter had set in, and by the first of December the oldest settlers were declaring they had never seen anything to equal it. The whole country was nearly snow-bound. Freighters were compelled to stop on their way between Buffalo and the railroad and abandon their outfits, and in many cases their stock died from exposure.

The poor range cattle. What of them? They were getting weak by the first of November, and by December were already beginning to die. They were wandering over the country in droves; now and then on some hill where the wind had blown off the snow they would find, maybe, a mouthful of grass. They were crowded in all the river and creek bottoms eating off the willow, sagebrush and greasewood. Under banks, and in all protected places, the poor things crowded to get a little protection from the bitter wind, which chilled their poor emaciated forms to the bone and froze lots of them to death in their sheltered places. They were compelled to keep moving in order to keep from freezing, and their feet were cut by the frozen snow until their trail could be followed by the blood which flowed from them.

In January there was a thaw that lasted for a day or two, melting the snow and the whole country was covered with slush and water. This was followed immediately by severe cold which froze the water and then the country was a slippery glacier which proved to be a veritable death trap for the weakened cattle. Whenever the poor animals would slip and fall they were too weak to ever get upon their feet again. The loss was fearful; thousands of cattle perished; but the full extent of the loss could not be determined until the spring round-up started.

There was one baron, though, who could figure his loss pretty accurately, . . . J. N. Tisdale. He had two years before bought a herd of 700 cows, paying $60 a head for them. The bunch, already considerably depleted by the preceding hard winter, was brought in to his ranch where he intended to feed them hay. The winter was so long and severe that he ran out of hay, and nearly 400 of these $60 cows died around his stables and were dragged off, and he hardly saved the rest by hauling hay a distance of 35 miles, for which he had to pay $25 a ton.

The first green grass of 1887 was welcomed with joy by both man and beast; for six long, dreary months the poor cattle had wandered from place to place, hunting for warmth and food, and the great wonder was how any one of them had lived.

Once more the barons are found in Cheyenne to consider the cheapest way to find out what they had lost during the winter. The cattle trust was formed. Some of the smaller outfits, such as Games and some outfits let their cattle to other larger outfits to run at so much per head, thus cutting down the number of wagons generally put out. The EK Co. turned its cattle in to the trust to be tallied out that summer. In previous years so anxious had parties been to buy cattle that they did not require them tallied out, but would buy them from the books. The round-up that spring was a small affair; from 27 wagons the spring of 1883, the number had gradually been reduced until only four were present in 1887.

5

CHEYENNE DAILY SUN

Two Notorious Characters Hanged for Cattle Stealing
1889

On July 20, 1889, James Averell and Ellen Watson were lynched near their ranches in Carbon County, Wyoming. Two days later, an article on the incident appeared in the Cheyenne Daily Sun, *a newspaper owned by an ally of the Wyoming Stock Growers Association. The writer justified the hangings by portraying Watson as a notorious prostitute and cow thief known as "Cattle Kate," a claim that would be repeated in many subsequent accounts. In deeming her a prostitute, a charge often leveled at women living alone in the West, the* Sun *helped legitimize the violence directed against her and Averell.*

Early yesterday morning a cowboy named Buchanan reached the ranch of E. J. Healy, forty miles west of Casper, and reported the lynching of Jim Averell and Ella Watson,[1] Saturday afternoon by stockmen. Averell kept a "hog" ranch at a point where the Rawlins and Lander stage road crosses the Sweetwater.[2]

Ella Watson was a prostitute who lived with him and is the person who recently figured in dispatches as Cattle Kate who held up a Faro dealer at Bessemer and robbed him of the bank roll. Both, it is claimed, have borne the reputation of being cattle rustlers and are believed to have been in league with Jack Cooper, a notorious cattle thief who died with his boots on in that vicinity a few months ago.

Buchanan said Averell started for Casper Saturday, accompanied by the woman and that they were taken from the wagon by a party armed at gun point on the Sweetwater, not far from the town of Bothwell and hanged from the summit of a cliff fronting the river. Buchanan, who was a friend of Averell, came upon the lynchers just after the woman

[1] Ella was Ellen Watson's nickname.
[2] A "hog ranch" was a frontier brothel.

"Two Notorious Characters Hanged for Cattle Stealing," *Cheyenne Daily Sun,* July 22, 1889, reprinted in George Hufsmith, *The Wyoming Lynching of Cattle Kate, 1889* (Glendo, Wyo.: High Plains Press, 1993), 212–15.

had been swung up and as they were in the act of hanging Averell. He fired at the lynchers, who returned the fire with interest and pursued him, but he had a good horse and managed to escape.

He claims to have identified several men, among them four of the most prominent stockmen in Sweetwater valley. Healy reached Casper last night and swore out warrants for the arrest of these men, and Deputy Sheriff Watson and a posse left at once for the scene of the tragedy.

The lynching is the outgrowth of a bitter feeling between big stockmen and those charged with cattle rustling. Every attempt on the part of the stockmen to convict thieves in the courts of that county for years has failed no matter how strong the evidence might be against them, and stockmen have long threatened to take the law into their own hands. This fact, together with the further one that Averell had had more or less trouble with every stockman in the section, probably accounts for the violent death of himself and the woman Watson.

Jim Averell has been keeping a low dive for several years and between the receipts of his bar and his women, and stealing stock he has accumulated some property. . . .

The story of the man's descent into the vile avocation which he pursued when justice overtook him is not a marvelous one. It is the old tale. A few words will suffice, a passion for gambling, for liquors and for lewd women carried him on to destruction.

6

JOHN H. FALES

Neither of Them Ever Stole a Cow

1955

The Cheyenne Daily Sun's *colorful portrayal of Ellen Watson as a fallen woman (Document 5) was reinforced by other chroniclers, such as John Clay (Document 7). However, a 1955 oral history interview with John H. Fales, a neighbor of the two victims, casts doubt on the "Cattle Kate"*

From "John H. Fales—Pioneer," transcript of 1955 interview by Robert B. David, David Collection, Casper College Library, Casper, Wyo.

legend. Fales's version is supported by public documents showing that Averell and Watson were secretly married and had filed separate adjacent homestead claims, a common practice among couples seeking larger homestead tracts in the arid West.

During my early days here I knew and was intimate with many interesting people. I knew Jimmy Averell and Ella Watson, better known as ["Cattle Kate"] well. In fact, my mother made the bonnet which Ella wore when she was hanged. And I built the cabin on Ella's homestead on Horse Creek. It was a single room, built of fir logs hauled by Jimmy Averell. It was fourteen by sixteen feet, had only one door, but there was a window in each side.

I know how Jimmy and Ella met in Rawlins where Jimmy had gone to file on his homestead which caused all the trouble later. Ella was working at the Rawlins house, and was at that time a fine appearing woman. She was large, being about six feet two inches tall and weighing about one hundred-sixty pounds. She was not only a fine appearing woman, but a good woman. Averell, in contrast to Ella Watson, was a small man.

He needed some one to run his road ranch, and he made this proposition to Ella: She was to take charge, and charge fifty cents a meal for all meals served there. Averell was to furnish supplies, and she could have what she made. Averell's homestead lay inside of Bothwell's pasture, land that he had fenced, but did not own. Later Ella Watson took up a homestead some nine miles away on Horse Creek, and above Bothwell's place.

Then she took out a water right and shut Bothwell off from water. It was this fact, and that fact that Averell had homesteaded Bothwell's pasture that brought on the trouble. It certainly wasn't any rustling operations of Averell's and Ella Watson's. Neither of them ever stole a cow. And those who say that Ella Watson slept with the cow-punchers, are slandering a good woman's name. She and Averell were engaged to marry, and were only waiting until she proved up on her homestead. She even adopted an eleven year old boy name[d] Decoy, because his home was not very pleasant.

As for her rustling cattle, she didn't. She bought her first bunch of twenty-eight head from an immigrant, named Engerman, at Independence Rock. The man was trailing through to Salt Lake and these cattle became foot sore. He sold them to Ella Watson for a dollar a head, and I drove them from Independence Rock to Averell's ranch.

Later, when the trouble over range arose, and Ella Watson and Jimmy Averell, accused of stealing cattle, were hung, the boy Ella had adopted, and Averell's fifteen year old nephew, nearly came to grief because of their relationship to these two. Some one at Bothwell's ranch sent these two boys two custard pies. Something made Averell's nephew suspicious, and he would not eat them. Later they were analyzed in Rawlins and enough strychnine was found in them to poison half the people in Wyoming.

7

JOHN CLAY

My Life on the Range

1924

Presenting the cattlemen's viewpoint, John Clay published his account in a 1924 autobiography, My Life on the Range. *Clay was a Scottish-born manager of a large ranching outfit in Carbon County in the 1880s, and he later went on to become president of the Wyoming Stock Growers Association. In this excerpt, he offers important background information explaining the cattlemen's frustration with rustling and their rationale for vigilante action, including the lynching of Ellen Watson and James Averell.*

Down the Sweetwater near to the Bothwell ranch a man of the name of "Jim" Averill [Averell] had started a roadhouse and saloon, and near by in a cabin lived Ella Watson known as "Cattle Kate." The yellow press, then very aggressive in the West, had written up this lady. She had ridden into Casper and from the pen of the scribes you would think she was a second Elizabeth visiting Leicester. As a matter of fact,

From John Clay, *My Life on the Range* (1924; repr., Norman: University of Oklahoma Press, 1962), 265–69.

she was a prostitute of the lowest type, and while Averill and a man called Buchanan were her intimates, she was common property of the cowboys for miles around. If they could not pay her the price of virtue in cash, they agreed to brand a maverick or two for her behoof. It was a kind of problem difficult to fathom, far less meet successfully. It was impossible to get a conviction if they were arrested even in the act.

One morning in the summer of 1889, after these parties had had repeated warnings that the objectionable class of business must stop, this man and woman were hanged. The man wilted and begged for mercy; the woman died game. This of course was a horrible piece of business, more especially the lynching of the woman, and in many ways indefensible, and yet what are you to do? Are you to sit still and see your property ruined with no redress in sight? This led on to two other parties disappearing, and it made matters worse in this sadly oppressed territory. While Henderson [George Henderson, manager of John Clay's ranch in Sweetwater] was not a party directly to this business, he was indirectly connected with it. In the fall of 1890 he was shot by a rustler at a small ranch a mile or two above the Three Crossings. His death was instantaneous. His murderer was convicted and sentenced to twenty years in prison, but he escaped through the influence of the jailer's daughter, so it is said.

When we first went to the Sweetwater Valley in 1882, about nine miles above the ranch on the river was a place called Rongis. It was run by Johnnie Signor as a road ranch and ginmill. Signor was a man of ability, and he gathered round him and influenced the worst element among the cowboys. All kinds of devilment were hatched in his saloon. One day there appeared among the brands of Wyoming passed by the brand commissioners what was known as the rocking chair brand, thus ⫫. Our brand was seventy-one quarter circle, 7ʟ. It was thus easily worked over by an expert cowman. The mavericks for miles around went into Signor's brand. At the roundups Signor was out large as life inspecting his property. The winter of 1886–87 trimmed his herd, but it kept increasing. Our herd, being in his vicinity, paid undoubtedly the heaviest toll. Henderson of course began to fight him and his satellites, and as out of the depleted herds there was not so much plunder to be made they could not do so much damage with the branding iron; but in other ways they were a thorn in the flesh.

One night in a spirit of revenge they sent down one, two, or more men who set fire to our haystacks and barn, and they went up in smoke. Everyone knew who did it. It was common talk. So Henderson and a stock detective who was with him put a match to Signor's haystacks, and there was a great bonfire. This stopped incendiarism [arson] in that neighborhood. The remedy was not legal, but it was effectual. When we moved away our herd, "Johnnie" also shifted his quarters into the Lost Cabin country west of Casper. This was not a congenial place for a man of his ideas of property. One day he disappeared. Dry-gulched[1] was the verdict of the neighbors, and some of them knew it personally. . . .

Put yourself, reader, in the place of those men whose herds had been cut in two in 1886–87, who were poor, discredited, in many cases disheartened, although they did not show it, and watch the steady aggression of the thief on their property, and then if you have the heart cast a stone at the men who made an effort to defend themselves.

Some thirty-three years ago (in the summer of 1891) Major Wolcott and I were walking across a beautiful alfalfa meadow on Deer Creek, a short distance from his house. . . . The subject of stealing on the range came up, and after a good deal of discussion the gallant major said there was urgent necessity for a lynching bee, especially in the northern part of the state, and he developed a plan he had in his mind.

At that time like many other cowmen I had thrown discretion to the winds, and was quite willing to draw a rope on a cattle thief if necessary, yet his scheme was so bold and open that I told him it was an impossible one, and that, so far as I was concerned, to count me out. After sleeping over it a night, I talked again to him, and strongly advised against any such action. I went away to Europe for a long holiday, and the matter left my mind. . . . I emphasize this because latterly I was accused of having planned and instigated the famous raid into Johnson County, whereas I was innocent as an unborn babe. From the time Wolcott spoke to me till I saw the telegraphic dispatch in the Irish paper I had not even a hint of the impending trouble. Further, I believe if I had been actively at work on the range that winter the famous "Johnson County invasion" would never have happened. Some of my associates were in it tooth and nail. One of them, C. A. Campbell, was of the party and every man in it made a band of the best, bravest men who ever lived.

. . . A quarter of a century changes people's ideas, and the passing of time gives time for reflection and mellows one's judgment. We are apt in these days to cry out loudly when an enraged population strings up some worthless brutal nigger who has raped some innocent woman,

---

[1]Fatally ambushed, typically from a dry gulch under a bridge.

and you will read the story of vigilance committees in early frontier days, more especially in San Francisco, with horror, and yet if you had lived in such times the critic of today would probably have been the performer of a faraway yesterday. In this world of complex conditions it is hard to define where law ends and individuality begins. Great reforms are brought about by revolutionary methods. The Boston Tea Parties, the victories of Washington were protests flung world-wide against a Teutonic dictator. The Chartists of 1848 are mild-mannered enthusiasts in the light of modern days.[2]

[2]The "Teutonic dictator" refers to Britain's George III. The Chartists were radical English political reformers who called for universal male suffrage, a secret ballot, and other measures that would broaden political participation.

8

ASA SHINN MERCER

The Banditti of the Plains

1894

Two years after the Johnson County War, Wyoming newspaper editor Asa Shinn Mercer published The Banditti of the Plains, *a scathingly critical view of the cattlemen's role in the conflict. In his book, he describes the killings of James Averell and Ellen Watson (referred to in this excerpt as "the Sweetwater executions"), as well as those of three other Johnson County residents who were "dry-gulched," or fatally ambushed, in 1891. Mercer's account of these killings illustrates the rising tensions around homesteading and cattle ranching in Johnson County and the growing popular resentment of large cattle owners and their vigilante campaigns.*

Emboldened by exemption from prosecution for the Sweetwater executions, the cattle ring determined to begin a systematic and indiscriminate slaughter of their supposed enemies. They had in their

From Asa Shinn Mercer, *The Banditti of the Plains* (1894; repr., Norman: University of Oklahoma Press, 1954), 20–27.

employ men of known recklessness and daring, and apparently the plan was to have these hired assassins begin on the eastern side of the state and pick off their men as they came to them. The first job was the hanging of [Tom] Waggoner, a few miles from Newcastle, on the morning of June 4th, 1891.

Three men went to his house and with false papers took him under arrest. He was alone with his wife and two small children, so his friends were ignorant of his arrest; in fact, his wife supposed he had gone with friends and quietly awaited his return, unsuspicious of foul play. The body was found on the 12th of June hanging to a tree in a gulch some miles away, since known as "Dead Man's Canyon." . . .

. . . Circumstances quite clearly pointed to certain men as the lynchers, but in Western parlance, they "had a pull," and no official action was taken. . . .

Orley E. Jones, familiarly known as "Ranger Jones," a young man of 23 years, went to Buffalo to arrange for lumber to complete his house on his claim, expecting to get married as soon as the building was ready for occupancy. He started home on the afternoon of the 28th, driving two horses to a buckboard. At the crossing of Muddy creek, fifteen miles out from town, he was shot three times by some one in hiding under the bridge. The wagon was taken to a gully some distance from the road, the horses turned loose and Jones' body left in the buckboard, the murderer or murderers seeking safety in flight.

J. A. Tisdale, who lived sixty miles from Buffalo, had gone in to purchase winter supplies for his family and, after a few days' visit, started home on the evening of the 30th, spending the night at the Cross H ranch, four miles out. Tisdale stated to friends in Buffalo that he had overheard Frank M. Canton tell Fred Hesse that he (Canton) would take care of Tisdale, and that he feared he would be killed on the road home. He was nervous and uneasy, and as a precaution bought a double-barrelled shotgun to carry. A local writer, speaking of this incident, says:

> . . . [Tisdale] started the next morning on his journey home. Three miles on his murderer was lying in a gulch within twenty feet of the road, waiting for his victim to approach. Slowly but surely Tisdale, with his heavy load, was going to meet his death at the hands of the cowardly fiend. He approached, passed, and when twenty-five feet by, the murderer's rifle belched forth its deadly contents. . . .

To avoid immediate discovery the wagon and team were driven half a mile below, the horses shot and the wagon and dead man left out of sight from the road. But Charles Basch, approaching from the south on horseback, had witnessed at least a part of the murderous deed, and he rode to Buffalo and gave notice of same. Basch charged Frank M. Canton with being the murderer. Sheriff Angus sent a deputy and a small posse after the body and it was taken to town. . . .

Canton was arrested and given a preliminary hearing before Justice of the Peace Parmalee. Two days were spent in the trial, when the accused was released.

The people freely charged the court with corruption and declared the evidence ample to justify the placing of the prisoner behind the bars without bail. Only the presence of cool heads in the community prevented the wreaking of vengeance upon Canton and some of his sympathizers. Canton and Hess left the state in a few days. Some time later, new and material evidence was found and a new information was filed. Canton was in the state of Illinois, and Governor Barber was asked to issue a requisition for his return. This request the governor refused. . . .

These cowardly shootings in the back from places of safety completed a list of dead at the hands of the cattle barons as follows: Jim Averill, Ella Watson, Tom Waggoner, O. E. Jones, and J. A. Tisdale, to say nothing of the attempts to murder, and yet they went unwhipped of justice, to plan and execute other forms of oppression and other methods of murder. No wonder the people of the state everywhere looked upon the cattlemen as being arrayed against them and as the enemies of true progress and development in the commonwealth. The eyes of the masses were opened to the situation.

9

SAM CLOVER

Riding with the Regulators

1892

Sam Clover was a reporter for the Chicago Herald *who covered the Indian wars and other western news. While working in the Chicago stockyards in 1891, Clover got a tip that Wyoming cattle owners were organizing a campaign against stock thieves. With a letter of introduction from a*

From Sam Clover, "Regulators in a Trap," *Chicago Herald*, April 16, 1892.

Chicago-based owner of a large cattle ranch in Johnson County, Clover made his way to Cheyenne the next spring and asked to join the expedition. Promising to present the cattlemen's point of view, Clover was admitted to the regulators' group that set out for Johnson County in April 1892. This article, published in the Herald *on April 16, is one of the few firsthand accounts of the violence at the KC and TA ranches.*

EDGEMONT, S.D., April 15—Ten days ago fifty men heavily armed with Winchesters and revolvers, representing the leading cattle interests in the northwest, met a rendezvous near the Casper mountains for the purpose of opening a campaign against the cattle thieves of Wyoming, to whom it was agreed no mercy should be shown and no quarter given. . . . In order that no news of the expedition should reach the headquarters of the rustlers at Buffalo, which point was to be taken by surprise and captured, the telegraph wire running from Fort McKinney to Douglas was cut in numerous places and rendered useless and hence the details of the adventures of the regulators have been slow in arriving. Scouts were sent ahead to take in all chance travelers who might get away and spread the alarm and in every way all possibility of leakage was guarded against. . . .

Night Ride in a Terrible Storm

With a blanket strapped behind each saddle and a lunch of crackers and bacon to last until the wagons should catch up, the mounted men dashed out of the camp in the face of a terrific snowstorm for an all-night ride to the middle fork of Powder river. . . .

For six hours horses and men breasted the fearful storm. . . . The frozen snow beat with savage violence against the exposed faces of the men, blinding their eyes so that it was impossible to see a foot beyond their horses' heads. . . . The determined men yet pushed ahead and at daybreak were within four miles of the ranch containing the thieves. Filing into a deep gulch, the regulators halted and dismounting rapidly built a number of fires from the abundant sagebrush, around which they formed for the purpose of thawing out before tackling the work at hand.

Lying Low for Rustlers

After an hour's rest and circulation being partially restored, the word was given to mount. In a few minutes the party was stretching in the direction of No Man's ranch.[1] Halting in the brush half a mile south of a house on the bank of the river, the regulators dismounted and from their number were chosen twelve men to make the attack. . . . The sharpshooters grasped their Winchesters and with revolvers buckled around their undercoats silently stole off in the direction of the ranch. Here they were advantageously placed by their leader so that every corner of the house was covered, and laying full length on their stomachs the regulators patiently awaited the appearance of the rustlers, the plan being to shoot them down as soon as they stepped outdoors.

Meantime the captain of the party with two others had stolen around to the stable which was about seventy-five yards north of the house. Here a discovery was made that threatened to disarrange the mode of attack. A buckboard and freighter's wagon were drawn up alongside the corral back of the stable and the presence of two strange teams proved conclusively that the rustlers were entertaining company over night. Whether they were thieves or merely chance freighters must be determined before a shot could be fired, as the regulators had no desire to steep their hands in innocent blood.

. . . After lying in the brush nearly two hours the firing party discerned some signs of life in the house, and presently an old man appeared, evidently one of the visitors who, tin bucket in hand, slowly sauntered down to the river to get water for breakfast. He was permitted to pass the stable unmolested, but the moment he was out of sight of the house two Winchesters were pointed at him and he was ordered to make no outcry. . . . Luckily for himself the old man soon satisfied his questioners that he was innocent and he also told them that the men they were after were still in bed, but his partner, another freighter was already up.

. . . The captain returned to his post to await the appearance of the second freighter. . . . It was fully half an hour before he sauntered forth. . . . On the same spot that the old fellow had been surprised the younger man was held up and he, too, was taken to the river bank and left in charge of a guard.

. . . The patience of the regulators was finally rewarded by the appearance of one of the thieves [Nick Ray], who stepped out of doors to gaze off in the direction of the river for the missing men. Barely had he come within range when crack, crack, crack went half a dozen Winchesters in rapid succession, and almost at the first shot the

---

[1] Clover is referring to the KC Ranch owned by John Nolan. Later in the article, he identifies it as Nolan's ranch.

rustler fell with a loud "—— you" emanating from his lips that could be plainly heard by the men posted behind the stable. But he was not killed, and with a great effort he started to crawl on all fours toward the open door a few feet away, when another shot took him in the back, and with a heavy groan he fell forward on the doorstep of the house, inside which he was rapidly dragged by his partner and the door was closed. . . .

Tackling a Desperate Outlaw

[Nate] Champion, the man that remained, was yet to be wiped out of existence. To do this the regulators knew would be no child's play. Brave as a lion, the best pistol shot in the country and with nerves like iron, he was not to be approached with impunity, as the regulators discovered when half a dozen shots fired from the window overlooking the stable and river whistled by some of the party that for an instant were unconsciously exposed. For a while the besiegers contented themselves with pouring hot shot into the house through the windows, but after wasting much valuable ammunition the leader of the party ordered his men to cease firing. . . .

Jack Flagg's Lucky Escape

While resting and discussing plans at the camp the road to the south was left entirely unguarded and it was during this time that a clumsy hay wagon drawn by a team of bay horses and driven by a lad of 16 pulled over the brow of the hill and passed within twenty yards of Champion's cabin. Behind the wagon rode a wiry-looking man mounted on a sorrel horse and wearing a black slouch hat. Just as he passed the regulators one of the latter pulled his Winchester on the rider who exclaimed: "Don't shoot, boys, I am all right," at the same time urging his horse to a sharper speed, successfully running the gauntlet of the eight men. He was about to cross the bridge when two new arrivals from the camp appeared, both of whom recognized in the escaping horseman one of the most desperate cattle thieves living in that section and a man above all others they wanted.

"Shoot the scoundrel! He's Jack Flagg!" they yelled, and at once began blazing away at the rustler, who put spurs to his animal and dashed away. . . . The boy in the wagon . . . seemed to grasp the situation in a glance, for rapidly cutting the harness, he leaped on the back of one of the horses he was driving, and abandoning the wagon sped off like the wind over the trail, followed closely by Jack Flagg. The shooting had, of course, aroused the men in camp, and looking across the river they saw the flying horsemen rapidly disappearing up the road. . . . In a few minutes ten men were in hot pursuit of Flagg and his companion, but the chase proved fruitless, and after following the daring rustlers three or four miles, they decided to turn back to camp, where they found the leaders of the expedition chewing the bitter quid[2] of chagrin and the entire party extremely disconcerted at this wholly unpardonable blunder.

Champion's Cabin Fired

That Flagg would ride north and arouse the country there could be no doubt. In place of a surprise the regulators felt they must be as prepared to meet with stubborn resistance, for all knew the rustlers to be men who would fight to a finish if they had the chance. . . . To get to Buffalo, sixty miles away as speedily as possible was instantly decided upon, but, enraged by the escape of Flagg, the leaders emphatically declared that Champion should be killed before they stirred a step. The hay wagon abandoned by the boy was quickly seized upon and drawn up in the rear of the stable, where it was filled with pitch pine, cottonwood logs, and hay piled high above the wheels, so that no bullets from Champion's unerring rifle could possibly reach those who were to back the wagon against the house.

Six men volunteered to steer the inflammable mass toward the shattered window through which so many bullets had penetrated, and with matches in their hands and with pistols drawn in case Champion should make a rush for liberty the men slowly backed the wagon toward the yawning aperture facing the river. During its progress a constant hail of bullets was poured in at the window by the sharp-shooters stationed for that purpose, thus precluding all possibility of Champion's firing upon the wagon party.

Plump against the window the combustible mass was lodged. Matches were instantly applied and in a few seconds the hay was ablaze. Then began a scamper back to cover the six volunteers. . . . No shots were fired, however, and the six men breathed easier as soon as the stable was reached. A strong wind was blowing from the river toward the house, and in a few minutes flame and smoke from the burning mass leaped in at the window. . . .

[2]Cud.

Shot Down as He Ran

The roof of the cabin was the first to catch on fire, spreading rapidly downward until the north wall was a sheet of flames. Volumes of smoke poured in at the open window from the burning wagon. . . . Still the doomed man remained doggedly concealed, refusing to reward them by his appearance. The cordon of sharpshooters stood ready to fire upon him the instant he started to run. Fiercer and hotter grew the flames . . . until every part of the house was ablaze and only the dug-out at the west end remained intact.

"Reckon the cuss has shot himself," remarked one of the waiting marksmen. "No fellow could stay in that hole a minute and be alive."

These words were barely spoken when there was a shout, "There he goes!" and a man clad in his stocking feet, bearing a Winchester in his hands and a revolver in his belt, emerged from a volume of black smoke that issued from the rear door of the house and started off across the open space surrounding the cabin into a ravine fifty yards south of the house, but the poor devil jumped square into the arms of two of the best shots of the outfit who stood with leveled Winchesters around the bend waiting for his appearance. Champion saw them too late, for he overshot his mark just as a bullet struck his rifle arm, causing the gun to fall from his nerveless grasp. Before he could draw his revolver, a second shot struck him in the breast and a third and a fourth found their way to his heart.

Nate Champion, the king of the cattle thieves, and the bravest man in Johnson county, was dead. Prone upon his back, with his teeth clinched and a look of mingled defiance and determination on his face to the last, the intrepid rustler met his fate without a groan and paid the penalty of his crimes with his life. A card bearing the significant legion, "Cattle thieves beware," was pinned to his blood-soaked vest, and there in the dawn, with his red sash tied around him and his half-closed eyes raised toward the blue sky, this brave but misguided man was left to lie by the band of regulators, who, having succeeded in their object, rapidly withdrew from the scene of the double tragedy. . . .

Following Champion's death a hearty supper was eaten, for by [this] time the wagons had come up in charge of the two cooks and a driver. . . . The horses were given a good supply of grain, harness[es] were tightly cinched, and at the command of "mount," the expedition drove off at a sharp trot, forty-seven strong headed straight for Buffalo, sixty miles away. . . . Thirty miles were made in five hours and here the outfit halted for a rest and to change horses, fresh animals being pressed into service at a big horse ranch. Again mounting the regulators sped on toward Buffalo, but at old Dick Carr's ranch at Crazy Woman Creek, the expedition received a temporary check at this point. Jack Flagg had succeeded in rustling about twenty men who were armed to the teeth, and in a narrow defile awaited the oncoming of the regulators. The accidental discharge of one of their guns revealed their presence, however, and averted what might have proved a Waterloo for the expedition[;] as it was the moment was a critical one. To go forward might mean death to many, to retreat was equally disastrous. . . . Rapidly swerving to the left, the party rode across the foothills, cut the wire fences on the Carr ranch, and by making a circuitous detour in an hour was enabled to strike the main traveled road again, leaving the enemy far in the rear. . . .

. . . At 9 o'clock the party had reached the T.A. ranch, twelve miles from their destination. Here the regulators were met by friends from Buffalo who rode out to strongly advise against going into town to make a fight, explaining that instead of thirty or forty men to oppose them there were already gathered upward of one hundred, with additional recruits pouring in from all quarters. Recognizing the folly of attempting to do battle against these odds, the leaders . . . determined to fall back on the T.A. ranch to rest the men and horses and to get some much-needed sleep. . . .

In the city of Buffalo, the seat of justice of Johnson county, the headquarters of the rustler element, the excitement was at fever heat. When on Sunday morning Jack Flagg rode into town with forty a sympathizer at his back to tell the story of his miraculous escape from Nolan's ranch, not knowing the result of the attack on Champion and Ray; he could only say the place was surrounded by a party of armed men. But an hour afterward a cowboy rode frantically up the main street of the town with the information that the Nolan ranch was fired and that he thought both of the occupants were killed.

Rustlers Wild for Revenge

This news drove the people fairly frantic and a hasty rush for guns and horses quickly ensued. Sheriff Angus, who is said to be in sympathy with the rustlers, started off with a posse of men to verify this statement, while another crowd of fully 150 armed riders and experienced fighters from Texas as leaders swept over the foothills of the Big Horn mountains toward the T.A. ranch, where the regulators were at once corralled and surrounded with little hope of escape.

10

OSCAR "JACK" FLAGG

The Siege at the TA Ranch

1892

Jack Flagg and his stepson's escape from the KC Ranch (Document 9) is described here by Flagg himself, who went on to alert nearby residents of Johnson County of the impending "invasion" of the regulators. Flagg, a local homesteader and ardent foe of the wealthy stock growers, recounts his efforts to recruit armed men to head them off and describes the ensuing siege at the TA Ranch, where the regulators took refuge. As hundreds of settlers surrounded the ranch, fighting between them and the regulators intensified, continuing for three days.

The morning of the 9th, I had started from my ranch, eighteen miles above the river, to go to Douglas. I was on horseback, and my stepson, a boy of 17 years of age, started with me to go to the Powder river crossing.

He was driving two horses and had only the running gear of a small wagon. We got to the KC ranch about 2:30 P.M. I was riding about fifty yards behind the wagon. We could not see the stable behind which the murderers were concealed, until we were within 75 yards of it. When the wagon drove into sight the murderers jumped up and commanded the boy to halt, but he urged up his horses and drove for the bridge. When they saw he would not stop, one of them took aim on the corner of the fence and fired at him. The shot missed him and scared his team, which stampeded across the bridge and on up the road.

There were 20 men behind the stable, and seven came up on horseback, three from one side of the road and four from the other, and closed in around me. When the men behind the stable saw me, they began to jump for their guns, which were leaning against the fence, and called on me to stop and throw up my hands.

From Oscar H. Flagg, *A Review of the Cattle Business in Johnson County, Wyoming, since 1892 and the Causes That Led to the Recent Invasion* (1892; repr., New York: Arno Press, 1969), 70–73.

I did not comply with their order but kept on straight for the bridge. When I got to the nearest point to them, 47 steps, a man whom I recognized as Ford, stepped from the crowd, and, taking deliberate aim at me with his Winchester, fired.

I threw myself on the side of my horse and made a run for it. The seven horsemen followed me. When I overtook my wagon, which had my rifle on it, I told the boy to hand it to me, which he did. I then told him to stop and cut one of the horses loose and mount him.

The seven horsemen were following me, and when I stopped, were 350 yards behind, but as soon as they saw I had a rifle, they stopped. I only had three cartridges for my rifle, and did not want to fire a one of them, unless they came closer, which they did not seem inclined to do.

The murderers then took the wagon we had left, pulled it back to the KC ranch, loaded it with pitch pine posts, shoved it against the house and set them afire, and the house was soon in flames.

After leaving the KC, we made our way to Trabing, 30 miles away, getting there at 9 o'clock at night. We were recruited with three more men, and started back to the assistance of the men who we thought were still imprisoned at the KC ranch.

We got to Carr's ranch, 17 miles from the KC and there we found 12 more men who had heard the news, it having been conveyed by Terrance Smith, who had heard the firing in the morning and hastened for Buffalo, scattering the news as he went.

Just as we rode up to Carr's ranch, some one exclaimed: "There they are on the flat, 100 strong." This was 12 o'clock at night. Just before we arrived at Carr's ranch the 12 men there had started to go to the KC and had seen the murderers coming and were preparing to ambush them, when one of the boys let his gun go off accidentally, and the murderers swung off to the left and went through Carr's field.

We laid at the ranch till daylight and then followed them up, passing them at the T.A. ranch, and going on to Buffalo. W. G. Angus had, in the meantime, started from Buffalo with a small squad of men for the KC, but we missed him on the way. We were reinforced in Buffalo and started back to the T.A. ranch with 48 men.

We surrounded the ranch at daylight, and a short while afterwards the invaders opened the fight by firing a shot at one of the squads of men about 400 yards off. That was a signal for hostilities to commence, which they did in earnest!

About nine o'clock, three wagons were described coming over the hill two miles away, and some of the boys started back and found them to be the invaders. They were taken possession of and pulled into camp and unloaded. Fuse, giant powder and poison were among the articles found in them. This was on Monday, April 11.

All day Monday recruits kept joining the besiegers, but the besieged were strongly fortified and it was impossible to rout them. The house was built of sawed logs 10 × 12 laid one upon the other. There were four rooms in the house. The windows were logged up and port-holes cut.

One hundred yards from the house was a log stable, and a short distance from the stable was a log fort, built on a hill that commanded a sweep of 600 yards in every direction. An ice house also made a good fort; all of these places were full of men with the finest kind of repeating rifles, that would carry up for a thousand yards.

Monday night was employed by the besiegers in digging rifle pits, and Tuesday morning they had approached considerably nearer the house.

Tuesday a large force of men joined the besiegers from both the Johnson and Sheridan counties. The construction of a movable fort was begun Tuesday and was ready to be moved up to the breastworks early Wednesday morning. Tuesday night the men worked like beavers. The invaders attempted to make a break for liberty Tuesday night and some of the horses were led out of the stable, but bullets were poured into them so fast and thick that they were glad to get back under cover.

Wednesday morning the situation was anything but pleasant for the invaders. The pits had been dug to within 300 yards of the house and the movable breastworks was ready to be moved forward; in fact it had been manned and was moving, when the bugles were heard and the soldiers came into sight, and in a few minutes the invaders had surrendered.

11

CHEYENNE DAILY LEADER

Time for Decided Action (Editorial)

1892

The Cheyenne Daily Leader *was one of the few major newspapers in Wyoming to denounce the invasion of the regulators. In this editorial, the writer defends the residents of Johnson County and offers a legal rationale for their actions while condemning those of Governor Amos Barber and the state government.*

However much each individual member of the stockmen's party may have been respected, however high their social or business standing or far-reaching their personal influence nobody can be blinded to the essential fact that with a band of armed mercenaries they were invading Johnson county to do violence to its inhabitants and commit crimes against the laws. In the present aspect of affairs it makes no difference as to the character and reputation of the men against whom they were proceeding. That an armed party had invaded their county was all that it was necessary for the constituted civil authorities and the people of Johnson county to know. It was then their duty as American citizens to rise up en masse and repel the invasion to the best of their ability. This they did not only with remarkable vigor but with an intelligence and military skill which surprised not merely the people of the state but of the country. The invading party was finally completely at the mercy of the civil authorities and citizens who besieged them, and they were rescued from inevitable capture and some of them perhaps from death by the interposition of the United States troops, and by that circumstance alone.

So far as this invasion is concerned, the law and equity up to this writing are entirely upon the side of the civil authorities and citizens of Johnson county. It was simply a piece of official presumption on the part of Gov. Barber to demand that the sheriff of Johnson county turn over to him the men captured by the civil authorities. . . .

From "Time for Decided Action," editorial, *Cheyenne Daily Leader*, April 17, 1892.

We do not for a moment believe the citizens there will seek a conflict with the United States authorities. During all their trouble they have shown coolness, common sense and a thorough grasp of the fundamental principles of the law. They have been provoked, and justly too, by the remarkable course pursued by Gov. Barber and his advisers. The official actions have been such as to lead not only them but every disinterested man in the state to believe that a conspiracy is on foot to thwart justice. They hear threats of martial law being applied to a community which has risen en mass[e] to uphold the law. . . .

Judging from what has already taken place we do not believe the people of Johnson county require anything more than a positive knowledge that justice will be done. So far they have every reason to believe the contrary. They believe the state authorities are leagued together to thwart justice. Let it be positively known before it is too late that this is not the case; that the only desire of the state government is to prevent the further sacrifice of human life and property and that justice must and shall prevail. Once the people are convinced of this they will go peaceably to their several homes, quietude will once again reign and the law may take its course in the usual regular way.

12

CHEYENNE DAILY SUN

It Is Tough (Editorial)

1892

The Cheyenne Daily Sun, *owned by a man who sympathized with the regulators, ran numerous articles supporting their campaign against rustlers in Johnson County. In this editorial, the* Sun *offers a defense of the regulators and argues that they should be released from custody. Later that summer, a Laramie County judge released the prisoners without bail.*

From "It Is Tough," editorial, *Cheyenne Daily Sun*, May 24, 1892.

Conceding a great deal to the rustlers it may be said the crime charged against the prisoners at Fort Russell is that they organized and attempted to redeem their property from thieves. A citizen who shoots down a burglar is praised. A wayfarer who sends a bullet into a footpad[1] is esteemed for the act. Men who repulse highwaymen are richly awarded. We submit then that the prisoners at the post are being treated infamously.[2] It seems to one watching closely the trend of events, that their greatest crime is failure. Had the expedition been a success how different would be the songs of thief sympathizers and the hell hounds scheming for political profit. This is a thing that has occurred in every new country. It is true that human life should be held in great value. It is equally true that a life more or less counts for little on the frontier. No great change is accomplished without bloodshed. In the movement under consideration a couple of thieves have been killed. One good honest man has been lost. A section is trembling and sleepless with fear. Murder is unbridled. Thieves and outlaws rule an entire subdivision of a state. They control absolutely and ply their vocation openly.

These then being the facts, we say it is tough that these men should continue restrained of liberty. They are guarded like felons. Their heavy interests are suffering to an extent that cannot be estimated. Thieves are reducing the herds daily. In the words of the unspeakable "Tommy" Gardner [an alleged rustler], "the rustlers have possession of that country and propose to keep it." To enumerate the outrages would require hours. To picture affairs in Johnson county as they exist is impossible. The condition is incredibly bad. Yet the men who own nearly all the property there is in Johnson county are held day after day and week after week to answer manufactured charges. It is tough.

[1] A highwayman; someone who robs pedestrians.
[2] Disgracefully.

13

F. A. MEREDITH

The Wyoming Cattle War

1892

In the summer of 1892, the Christian Union, *a reform-minded weekly newspaper in New York, published a series of articles offering different points of view on the Johnson County War. F. A. Meredith, managing editor of the* Rocky Mountain News *in Denver, contributed the last article in the series. In it, he attempts to situate the conflict within the larger historical context of the ranching frontier.*

The Wyoming cattle troubles originated in a palpable conflict of interests between the range cattle-growing business and the rights of actual settlers under the homestead or pre-emption laws. These two interests have never existed harmoniously in the same territory, and in the nature of things they cannot. It is a menace to the small farmer to have herds of cattle numbered by thousands roaming at will over the ranges. It requires fences of extra strength to secure his crops, and it costs both vigilance and hazard to avail himself of the outside grazing for his few head of stock, because they are liable to be swept off in the great herds, with small hope of recovery.

Hitherto this conflict of interests has always resulted in favor of the settler, because the law is on his side. The fact that such friction has invariably been followed by the withdrawal or breaking up of the large herds, as witness the experience of western Nebraska and Kansas and eastern Colorado, has doubtless emphasized the hostility of the large cattle companies towards the presence of settlers upon territory which they had been accustomed to use as grazing ranges. Whether this hostility has been authorized or not, it has undoubtedly been expressed by the employees of the large companies, and has resulted in many annoyances to settlers, and in giving rise to mutual bitterness. . . .

From F. A. Meredith, "The Wyoming Cattle War," *Christian Union*, August 13, 1892, 7.

On the one hand, many pioneer settlers, in the main noted for their rugged honesty, became so alienated in sympathy from the range cattle-owners because of persecutions, more or less serious, that they learned to regard with indifference the depredations of thieves upon the large herds, and juries of these settlers in some instances refused to convict, although the evidence of guilt was declared to be conclusive by the presiding judge.

On the other hand, the cattlemen, while suffering grievous wrong from professional cattle-thieves, failed to sufficiently discriminate between such characters and settlers who depended upon their own labor for a livelihood, whose worst fault arose from having had their moral sensibilities blunted by the aggravating conditions that prevailed. The whole population of that section was unjustly stigmatized by newspapers published in the interest of the leading cattle-owners, and a law was passed empowering a commission to seize the purchase money of all shipments of stock from Wyoming the title of which an agent of the commission might choose to suspect, and hold the same until the owner or ostensible owner of the stock should go to Cheyenne and prove his title to the satisfaction of the commission. This law has worked a hardship to settlers who are also cattle-growers on a small scale, and the charge has been freely made, and is generally believed by the rural population of Wyoming, that the law was enacted to deter the agricultural settlement of the State, that the use of the ranges for the grazing of large herds might be prolonged. . . .

The reception given the invaders by the people of Johnson County is explained by the conditions referred to at the commencement of this article. The belief was general that the purpose was indiscriminate murder and the destruction of property, and not merely the killing of persons known to have branded cattle unlawfully. Upon no other theory can we account for the uprising *en masse* for the purpose indicated of a rural population, old and young, that will average with any other pioneer population in the country in sterling qualities. Moreover, the same belief was entertained by the people of adjoining counties, who have, since the unfortunate occurrence, been practically unanimous in sustaining the people of Johnson County. . . .

The range cattle industry—by which is meant vast herds of cattle roaming over the plains, and relying, winter and summer, upon the product of Government lands for their subsistence—ceases to be a legitimate business when it comes in conflict with the homesteader and his rights. That point has been reached in Wyoming.

14

OFFICERS OF THE NINTH CAVALRY

The Suggs Affair

1892

Following the surrender of the vigilantes at the TA Ranch, angry residents in Johnson County engaged in retaliatory violence and vandalism, and a U.S. deputy marshal aligned with the stock growers was murdered that May. The state's cattlemen called on the governor and federal officials to declare martial law and send in new troops. In early June 1892, President Benjamin Harrison dispatched the Ninth Cavalry to Suggs, Wyoming, a railroad camp just north of Johnson County. Known as buffalo soldiers, the members of the Ninth Cavalry were all African Americans. These units serving in the West were primarily charged with fighting Indians, capturing Mexican bandits, and intervening in social conflicts such as mining and range wars. Often called on to defend western property interests against miners and homesteaders, the buffalo soldiers became lightning rods for popular discontent and racism, which resulted in repeated conflicts with white settlers. In Johnson County, their presence prompted class and racial resentments that led to violence. On June 17, a gunfight in Suggs left one soldier dead and two wounded. A board of officers convened to investigate the incident filed the following report.

The town of Suggs, Wyo., is situated on Powder River about 5 miles below the encampment of this command, consisting of six troops of the 9th U.S. Cavalry. The inhabitants of the town are composed of two distinct elements, the towns people proper, and a floating population called rustlers, whose sympathies are with recent movement against the cattlemen in this State, and which is made up of the worst types of western life.

Immediately upon the arrival of the 9th Cavalry in this vicinity it was perceived by both officers and men that while the first element was peaceably disposed, the second was in an ugly mood and viewed their

---

From Captain John S. Loud, Captain John F. Guilfoyle, and First Lieutenant A. B. Jackson, Ninth Cavalry, "Report on Suggs Disturbance, June 18, 1892," in *Wyoming Flames of '92*, ed. George D. Heald (Oshoto, Wyo.: n.p., 1972), xcii–xcvii.

arrival with distrust and hostility. These feelings were undoubtedly intensified by race prejudice, and probably also by the knowledge of the presence in the 9th Cavalry camp of one Philip Du Frand, whose life they had repeatedly threatened, and who was an active agent of the cattlemen's party. The animosity on the part of the rough characters of the town was shown by their following officers and enlisted men, who were present in town to make necessary purchases, from store to store, and by dropping insulting remarks in their hearing.

On the evening of June 16 two members of the 9th [Cavalry], Private Smith, Troop G, and Private Champ, Troop G, visited the town, the former mounted, for the purpose of posting advertisements for proposals for freighting for this encampment; the latter dismounted, was there without authority. There were present in the town at this time a number of prostitutes who had been intimately known by members of the 9th Cavalry while stationed at Fort McKinney, Wyo., and elsewhere; the action of these women in receiving the soldiers served still further to increase the hard feelings already engendered, and on the evening in question when Private Champ attempted to enter the house occupied by one of these women, the act was resented, a few moments later in a neighboring saloon by her white lover at the point of a revolver. The assailant was immediately covered by a revolver in the hands of Private Smith, who was in turn covered by several revolvers in the hands of bystanders. The combatants were separated by the bartender in whose saloon the occurrence took place, and both sides left the building.

The two soldiers were then conducted in a detour to the edge of the town by the bartender, who warned them that they might be waylaid. On arriving here both troopers mounted Private Smith's horse and started for this camp; on leaving the town they were fired upon by parties concealed in some houses on the outskirts. Both escaped, Private Smith with a bullet through his hat, and returning the fire with their revolvers, hastened to camp. Their arrival here was the occasion of great excitement among the troops who at once wanted to go in a body to the town.

The guard was formed and the number of sentinels around camp increased. Through the efforts of the troop officers and of the Commanding Officer, the men were finally calmed and after giving assurance that they would not visit the town without authority from their officers, went quietly to their tents.

On the next morning, June 17, the excitement seemed to have wholly subsided; everything went on as usual, and there was no apprehension of any further trouble growing out of the affair. The Commanding Officer during the day had the necessary supplies purchased and the mail carried to and from town by civilian teamsters in the employ of the government instead of by soldiers as heretofore. At night as a precautionary measure the sentries around camp were doubled, and two check roll-calls were ordered, one at 11 o'clock P.M., and the other at 1 o'clock A.M., both to be under the supervision of an officer in each troop.

At 10:30 o'clock P.M., distant firing was heard in the direction of the town and the command was at once formed under arms. The result of the roll call showed three non-commissioned officers and 39 privates absent; some of the privates it was afterwards found had not left camp. All the troop horses and mules were found to be present. It was evident at once that in spite of the precautions taken by the Commanding Officer, the night being very dark, some of the men had slipped through the chain of sentries and gone dismounted to retaliate for the hostile act of its inhabitants by terrorizing the town.

Two troops of Cavalry were at once dispatched under command of Captain J. F. Guilfoyle to ascertain the cause of the disturbance, protect the inhabitants if necessary, and render such assistance as was in his power. The remaining four troops were formed in a skirmish line around the camp to protect it if necessary and intercept the return of the absentees. These soon began to arrive, some had been engaged in the disturbance, and others had not reached there until after the affair was over; they were all at once put under guard.

Captain Guilfoyle's command was accompanied by a Doctor and an ambulance, and on the way to the town, met two returning soldiers, Private William Champ, Troop G, 9th Cavalry, and Captain William Tompkins, Troop G, Ninth Cavalry; both were wounded, the former in the shoulder and the latter in the hand, but neither seriously. On arriving in town, one soldier, Private Willis Johnson, Troop I, Ninth Cavalry, was found dead in the street, having been shot through the head, and one rustler, Bennett by name, wounded in the arm. Diligent inquiry disclosed the fact that about twenty soldiers penetrated through the center of the town and fired one volley in the air, and then commenced firing through the street and at some of the houses. At the first volley, a number of rustlers rushed to a neighboring saloon called the "Rustlers' Headquarters" and opened fire with their Winchesters, in which they were assisted by the inhabitants of the town from different houses. This fire was returned by the soldiers who then withdrew.

After bringing back those of the inhabitants that had fled from the town, and restoring confidence by the protection afforded by the presence of the troops, Captain Guilfoyle's command early the next morning returned to this camp. The remains of Private Johnson were brought back and interred here this afternoon. After consultation with the Doctor, and a careful examination of the holes in the dead man's

hat the Board is of the opinion that Private Johnson was shot from
behind, but whether by the Rustlers or by members of his own party
in the excitement of the melee, could not be ascertained.

It is the opinion of the Board that while the primary and exciting
cause of the trouble came from the part of the Rustlers, the occurrence of the night of June 17 was a retaliatory act on the part of about
20 of the soldiers, and one in which they took the initiative. The ringleaders on the part of the troops were Private Smith, Troop E, 9th
Cavalry, and Private Champ, Troop G, 9th Cavalry, who are mainly
responsible for the trouble.

> Signed: John S. Loud, Capt. 9th Cavalry, President
> Jno. F. Guilfoyle, Capt. 9th [Cavalry], Member
> Alfred B. Jackson, 1st Lt., 9th Cavalry, Recorder

15

ASA SHINN MERCER

The Trial of the Invaders
1894

*Asa Shinn Mercer was the author of the best-known early account of the
Johnson County War,* The Banditti of the Plains, *published in 1894.
Born in Illinois in 1839, Mercer migrated to Washington Territory in
1861, then moved to Texas, where he entered the newspaper business,
acting as editor and publisher of five Texas papers. In 1883, he settled in
Cheyenne, Wyoming, and took over as editor of the* Northwestern Livestock Journal, *the chief organ of the state's large cattle owners. After the
Johnson County War, which Mercer publicly opposed, he had a falling-out
with his former clients. Two years later, he published a scathing account
of the conflict, depicting the large stock owners as "assassins" and equat-
ing them with the legendary* banditti *who terrorized rural Italy. In this
excerpt, he describes the trial of the regulators and the final disposition of
the case, which left many Johnson County residents deeply dissatisfied.*

From Asa Shinn Mercer, *The Banditti of the Plains* (1894; repr., Norman: University of
Oklahoma Press, 1954), 127–33.

On August 7, 1892, the invaders were arraigned before Judge Scott, in the District Court for Laramie county, at the courthouse at Cheyenne. They all pleaded not guilty, and the work of securing a jury began. Three days were consumed and some progress made. It was evident that a jury could be found in the county, and hopes began to be entertained that the prisoners would be called upon to face their accusers for the killing of Nathan D. Champion and Nick Ray, and the burning of the Nolan ranch on Powder river, April 9, 1892. Skeptics and doubters there had been from the time of the arrest of the prisoners. "They never will be tried," was an expression heard every day, and in all parts of the state. The theory was that the cattlemen exerted such a dominating influence that in some way they would prevent a final hearing and that the accused would go free. The special privileges granted the prisoners throughout the summer months strengthened this idea, but when the day of trial came and both prisoners and witnesses appeared in court, the doubters began to hope that they were mistaken in their judgment.

But a bomb shell was already loaded, with fuse attached. At the close of the third day the sheriff, A. D. Kelly, presented a petition to Judge Scott for relief, setting forth that Johnson county was bankrupt; that its officials had not paid the expenses incurred by the detention of the prisoners in Albany county pending the hearing on the motion for a change of venue; that the cost of holding the prisoners, including hall rent, guards and food, was over a hundred dollars a day; that he could not get any money from the county officials with which to meet these bills; that Johnson county warrants would not take the place of money; that he, as sheriff, would no longer assume responsibility for these current expenses, and praying for an order of court that would secure him against loss as he could no longer hold the accused.

When court convened on the morning of August 10th Judge Scott handed down his decision on the above named petition in substance as follows:

I am unable to issue an order compelling Johnson county to make good the sheriff's disbursements for the maintenance of the prisoners, and as he has refused to longer provide for them, my only alternative is to admit them to bail. But as the defense refuse to furnish bail, I am forced to release them on their individual recognizances.

The prisoners at once signed each his own bail bond for $20,000 in the two separate cases, and they were all set at liberty, but ordered to appear at the next term of court, in January, 1893.

When this news reached the public a feeling of disgust was everywhere manifest, save among the white caps [regulators], who flung
their banners on the outer walls and literally colored the town crimson. It was then clearly demonstrated that the old guard had gotten in
its work, and that crime was still to go unwhipped of justice. . . .

Thoughtful persons asked why Governor Barber had brought these
men hundreds of miles from the scene of their misdeeds to be held at
the expense of Johnson county, and ready money demanded at every
turn in the case? Johnson county's credit was good at home and
abroad—her warrants had always been paid and her people would have
been glad to furnish guards and provisions for the invaders and taken
their pay in evidences of indebtedness, knowing that they were good for
their face value. This privilege was denied them, and the costs more than
doubled by transferring the case to distant points for a hearing. Beside
this the white cap press continually held Johnson county up as a bankrupt community and insisted that it could never pay the cost of a trial.
This tended to weaken or destroy her credit away from home and rendered the borrowing of money difficult. Looking at the train of circumstances as a whole, and connecting them with the final release of the
prisoners without trial, on the plea of Johnson county bankruptcy, the
consensus of opinion in many circles was that the 10th of August witnessed the closing act of a drama (if such a comparison may be allowed)
fully outlined before the prisoners left Fort McKinney for Cheyenne
under military escort. The fact that confidence in their ultimate release
never seemed to be lacking in the minds of the invaders strengthens this
view of the case. They apparently knew what was to be the outcome.

There were many ludicrous and humiliating incidents connected
with the detention and partial trial of these men. They were under
arrest for murder, in the hands of the law and the sheriff; yet when
arraigned in court to plead, F. M. Canton was carried in on a stretcher,
wounded by the accidental discharge of his own pistol while in one of
the city saloons in the early morning hours. This was made the
excuse for asking an order of court to disarm the prisoners, and as
there was a living example of the danger before the court, the order
was granted. This was the 7th day of August, and the prisoners had
been in custody since April 13—all this time carrying the arms and
flaunting them in the face of the law, while the citizens walked the
streets with no weapons of defense. . . .

Immediately on the signing of their bonds, preparations commenced for leaving the city. The Texans and many of the cattlemen
took the afternoon train for the East. The fiscal agents of the Stock

Association were part of the outgoing throng, which laid over a day in Omaha to settle up with the hired men. These were supposed to be on the payroll at $5 a day from the time of their enrollment in March up to the hour of their discharge by the court, as well as for the computed time of their journey home. The Omaha papers of the 12th and 13th of April announced the happy adjustment of these financial arrangements and the departure of the late imprisoned on their way south in the best of spirits and with canteens well filled.

Tom Smith, the captain of the Texans, has since paid the last penalty. He was shot and killed by a Negro desperado on the [railroad] cars between Gainesville, Texas, and Guthrie, Oklahoma, in the summer of 1893. Others of the band are reported killed, but how many is not known. He who lives by the sword shall perish by the sword, will no doubt prove true with many of these reckless characters.

A goodly number of the cattlemen quietly departed for a change of air, while others repaired to their respective places of domicile. . . .

January 21, 1893, when the case of the State of Wyoming vs. the Invaders was called, nearly all of the cattlemen responded but the hired men failed to appear. Alvin Bennett, prosecuting attorney for Johnson county, offered a motion to enter a nolle prosque,[1] to which the attorneys for the defense entered an objection. After discussion the court accepted the motion and the prisoners were discharged. A similar motion was made covering the cases of the hired Texans, who had not appeared, and an order of discharge was entered in the court records, also one rescinding the order of forfeiture of bail bonds previously entered.

This action was sever[e]ly criticized by many as unwarranted and outrageous, but the public finally settled down to the common opinion that the ring had so many obstructions of one kind and another to spring that justice was not likely to be meted out in the event of a long and expensive suit, and perhaps it was as well to end the farce without further cost to Johnson county settlers. It presented one object lesson that would in the end result in good to the state by arousing a sentiment among the masses in opposition to corporation rule that in future would prevent similar disgraces.

---

[1] Nolle prosequi; a declaration that the case will be dropped.

16

The Invasion Song
1890s

"The Invasion Song" was penned by an unknown author in Buffalo, Wyoming, shortly after the conclusion of the Johnson County War. One of several folk ballads written after the conflict, "The Invasion Song" was a testament to the widespread popular appeal of the settlers' cause. According to musicologists, the song was still being sung in Wyoming in the mid-twentieth century. By contrast, no balladeer seems to have taken up the cattlemen's side. The Johnson County War would go on to achieve a mythic status as it became the subject of numerous western novels and Hollywood films.

Sad and dismal is the tale I now relate to you,
'Tis all about the cattlemen, them and their murderous crew.
They started out on their manhunt, precious blood to spill,
With a gang of hired assassins, to murder at their will.

God bless poor Nate and Nick, who gave their precious lives,
To save the town of Buffalo, its brave men and their wives.
If it hadn't been for Nate and Nick, what would we have come to?
We would have been murdered by Frank Canton and his crew.

Poor Nate Champion is no more, he lost his precious life,
He lies down in the valley, freed from all care and strife.
He tried to run the gauntlet, when they had burned his home,
And Nick was lying lifeless, lips wet with bloody foam.

The run was made; his doom was sealed, a fact you all know well.
They left his lifeless body there, on the slope above the dell.
No kindred near to care for him, to grasp his nerveless hand;
A braver man was never faced, by Canton's bloody band.

"The Invasion Song," reprinted in Ariel A. Downing, "Music as Artifact: The Johnson County War Ballads," *Annals of Wyoming* 70 (Winter 1998): 21. Reprinted from Olive Wooley Burt, *American Murder Ballads* (New York: Oxford University Press, 1958), 172–74.

The very next name upon the list, was that of brave Jack Flagg.
Frank Canton must have surely thought, that he would "fill his bag."
Jack and his stepson came in view, a-riding 'round the curve;
"Throw up your hands! By God, they're off!" Frank Canton lost his
    nerve.

"Red Angus" next, the "canny Scot," was marked for Canton's lead.
But Angus, warned by bold Jack Flagg, for aid and succor sped.
The countryside now swarmed to life, the settlers armed in haste;
Soon "Red" had hundreds at his back, who Canton's minions faced.

To Crazy Woman's winding bank, the cowed invaders fled,
With KayCee [KC] blazing in their rear and Ray and Champion dead.
Here, held at bay, the cravens halt, 'till soldiers came to aid;
And now, secure in jail they rest, the debt of blood unpaid.

2

The Colorado Coal Strike

17

UNITED MINE WORKERS OF AMERICA, DISTRICT 15

Strike Resolutions

1913

On August 16, 1913, United Mine Workers of America (UMWA) organizer Gerald Lippiatt was killed in a dispute with Baldwin-Felts Agency detectives in downtown Trinidad, Colorado. Workers' outrage over the killing acceler- ated organizing efforts over the next month, prompting a mass turnout at the September UMWA convention in Trinidad. On September 16, Mother Jones delivered a rousing speech urging the workers to strike, and soon after, the delegates approved the following strike resolutions.

We, the representatives of the Mine Workers of District 15, after repeated efforts to secure a conference with the operators for the pur- pose of establishing joint relations and a fair wage agreement, and having been denied such a conference, the operators ignoring our invitation entirely, and believing as we do that we have grievances of great moment that demand immediate adjudication, we submit the fol- lowing as a basis of settlement:

First   We demand recognition of the Union.

Second   We demand a ten per cent advance in wages on the tonnage rates and the . . . day wage scale. . . . We also demand a ten

From "Proceedings: Special Convention of District Fifteen United Mine Workers of America Held in Trinidad, Colorado, 16 September 1913," Edward Doyle Papers, Denver Public Library.

per cent advance on the wages paid coke oven workers, and on all other classes of labor not specified herein.

Third   We demand an eight-hour work day for all classes of labor in and around the coal mines and at coke ovens.

Fourth   We demand pay for all narrow work and dead work, which includes brushing, timbering, removing falls, handling impurities, etc.

Fifth   We demand checkweighm[e]n[1] at all mines to be elected by the miners without any interference by Company officials in said election.

Sixth   We demand the right to trade in any store we please, and the right to choose our own boarding place and our own doctor.

Seventh We demand the enforcement of the Colorado Mining Laws and the abolition of the notorious and criminal guard system which has prevailed in the mining camps of Colorado for many years.

[1]Men to check the weight of the coal mined by each worker. Miners were paid by weight, but the company often underweighed the coal.

18

GEORGE P. WEST, U.S. COMMISSION ON INDUSTRIAL RELATIONS

Report on the Colorado Strike

1915

The federal Commission on Industrial Relations was established by the U.S. Senate in 1912 in response to growing labor-capital violence, including several recent bombings and killings in western states. Fearing that these conflicts might lead to revolution, a group of prominent intellectuals and social reformers called on the government to investigate industrial relations and propose solutions. President Woodrow Wilson appointed a

From George P. West, U.S. Commission on Industrial Relations, *Report on the Colorado Strike* (Washington, D.C., 1915), 15, 34–35, 38, 45–47, 53–59, 61–64, 67–68, 70, 73, 78–80, 82–83.

Missouri labor attorney, Frank Walsh, as chair of the commission along with eight other representatives of business, labor, and the public. Following the public outcry over the Ludlow tragedy in April 1914, the commission conducted hearings in 1914–1915 on the Colorado coal strike, resulting in three volumes of published testimony and a 190-page report. The first half of the report, excerpted here, examines the causes of the strike as well as living conditions in the Colorado coal camps.

The Colorado strike was a revolt by whole communities against arbitrary economic, political and social domination by the Colorado Fuel & Iron Company and the smaller coal mining companies that followed its lead. This domination has been carried to such an extreme that two entire counties of southern Colorado for years have been deprived of popular government, while large groups of their citizens have been stripped of their liberties, robbed of portions of their earnings, subjected to ruthless persecution and abuse, and reduced to a state of economic and political serfdom. Not only the government of these counties, but of the state, has been brought under this domination and forced or induced to do the companies' bidding, and the same companies have even flouted the will of the people of the nation as expressed by the President of the United States.

Economic domination was achieved by the Colorado Fuel & Iron Co. and its followers through the ruthless suppression of unionism, accomplished by the use of the power of summary discharge, the black list, armed guards, and spies, and by the active aid of venal state, county and town officials, who placed the entire machinery of the law at the disposal of the companies in their persecution of organizers and union members. . . .

That the leading mine owners were, in fact, ignorant of the conditions under which the miners and their families worked and lived, is clearly established by the evidence. Mr. Rockefeller, Jr., the most influential single owner, had not visited Colorado for ten years, at the time of the strike, nor had he attended a directors' meeting during that period. Testifying before the Congressional Committee and before this Commission, he said that he had "not the slightest idea" of what wages the miners received, of what rent the company charged them for their houses, or of other details vitally affecting their welfare. . . .

In Colorado the executive officials of the Colorado Fuel & Iron Company, and the owners and officials of the other leading companies, maintained their offices in Denver, 200 miles north of the mines, which they seldom visited. Neither Mr. Bowers nor Mr. Welborn[1] was charged with the actual operation of the mines, and knew little about this part of the business. Operations were in charge of Mr. Weitzel, manager of the fuel department, whose headquarters were at Pueblo, still many miles from the mining camps. . . .

Thus there existed a condition wherein all personal relationship and personal responsibility vanished at some point in the long procession of intermediaries standing between the miner in his room underground, and the directors and owners in New York. His personal contact seldom got beyond the foreman or pit boss, himself responsible for results to a superintendent, who in turn was responsible to an assistant manager, and so on up the scale until the needs and aspirations and well-being of 6,000 miners and their families ceased to exist as pressing realities for the responsible officials whose word was law in these communities. . . .

That the operators of southern Colorado denied their men the right of collective bargaining, is admitted. They refused to enter into conference or negotiation with officials of the only labor organization to which their men could have belonged, and insisted that they alone must determine wages and working conditions, dealing with each miner as an individual, and giving him no recourse if he became dissatisfied, except to quit his employment, pack his belongings, and with his family leave his home and community to seek work elsewhere. . . .

With no strong union in the field to limit their power to discharge without cause, the Colorado Fuel & Iron Company had used this power to build up a powerful political machine for the absolute control of town and county government and the partial control of the state government. This control was in turn used to keep out union organizers and to break strikes. Thus a vicious circle was drawn, industrial control leading to political control, and political control maintaining industrial control. How the company's political domination was achieved is described with great frankness in the following letter from Mr. Bowers to Mr. Charles O. Heydt, secretary to Mr. Rockefeller, Jr. It is dated May 13, 1913:

> The Colorado Fuel and Iron Company for many years were accused of being the political dictator of southern Colorado, and in fact were

[1]L. M. Bowers, chief executive of Colorado Fuel and Iron, and Jesse F. Welborn, president of the company.

a mighty power in the entire state. When I came here it was said that the C. F. & I. Co. voted every man and woman in their employ without any regard to their being naturalized or not; and even their mules, it used to be remarked, were registered if they were fortunate enough to possess names. . . .

Since I came here not a nickel has been paid to any politician or political party. We have fought the saloons with all the power we possess. We have forbidden any politician from going into our camps, and every subordinate official connected with the company has been forbidden to influence our men to vote for any particular candidate. We have not lobbied in the Legislature, but have gone directly to the Governor and other able men and have demanded fair treatment.

Mr. Bowers' assurance that the company had relinquished its political control some time prior to May 13 is disproved by a great deal of conclusive testimony, including letters and testimony by Mr. Bowers himself. . . .

While the testimony and letters quoted above throw much light on the methods by which political control was obtained by the companies, they do not set forth with entire clearness two of the principal sources of the companies' power. These are the right to discharge summarily and without stated cause; and the private ownership, by the companies, of every foot of land and of every building in many of the largest mining towns.

The operators have admitted freely that men would not be accepted or retained in their employ who talked unionism or who answered the operators' description of "agitators." To detect employees who were objectionable to the company, spies were employed and a system of espionage maintained. . . .

Free speech in informal and personal intercourse thus was denied the inhabitants of the coal camps. There is conclusive testimony that it also was denied to public speakers. Obviously, union organizers would not be permitted to enter the camps and address meetings. The Reverend Mr. Gaddis, head of the sociological department of the Colorado Fuel & Iron Company before and during the strike, testified that periodicals permitted in the camps were censored in the same fashion.

Thus, with "cut-throats" employed as spies to ferret out employees expressing objectionable opinions, the operators were able to use their power of summary discharge to deny free speech, free press and free assemblage, to prevent political activity contrary to their interests, and affirmatively to control the political activities of employees for the suppression of popular government and the winning of political control.

But in the Colorado camps the loss of his job was not the only penalty that might be arbitrarily inflicted on the miner who refused to do the company's bidding. Many of the mining towns were situated on land owned by the employing company. No bit of ground and no house could be occupied except by consent of the company, which discouraged home-building and refused to sell lots for the purpose, even to their oldest employees. The fact that some of the closed camps have flourished for thirty years disposes of the operators' claim that home ownership by the miners would be impracticable and unprofitable. In these towns, of which the names of twelve were given by Mr. Welborn as the property of the Colorado Fuel & Iron Company alone, the company owns not only the miners' dwellings, but the church, school, store, and saloon buildings. . . .

Thus employees were forced not only to depend on the favor of the Company for the opportunity to earn a living, but to live in such houses as the Company furnished, to buy such food, clothing and supplies as the Company sold them, to accept for their children such instruction as the companies wished to provide, and to conform even in their religious worship to the Company's wishes.

Under these conditions, the miner who was discharged by the pit boss or superintendent lost his house and his right to remain in the community at the same time that he lost his employment. . . .

Even the polling places in the closed camps were located on ground owned by the Company. If the votes of their employees were not sufficiently numerous to offset those of outsiders in the same precinct, entrance to the closed camps and the polling places could be denied to voters not under the Company's control, or the territory could be reprecincted in such fashion as to exclude these voters. . . .

Having described the methods by which political control was obtained, this report will now outline those uses of this power that have a direct bearing on industrial conditions. These were the disregard of state mining laws; the prevention of legislation unfavorable to the companies; the obtaining of favorable legislation; the control of coroners and courts; and the control of sheriffs, constables and militia. . . .

Testimony from union officials, strikers and apparently unbiased witnesses before the Congressional Committee and the Commission on Industrial Relations all points to the existence of a system of policing by company agents which closed the mining towns to union organizers, active members of the union, and, in fact, to any person whom the local authorities regarded as undesirable. A federal grand jury which met at Pueblo early in the strike and which heard testimony from a large number of witnesses had the following to say in its report:

> Many camp marshals, whose appointment and salaries are controlled by local companies, have exercised a system of espionage and have resorted to arbitrary powers of police control, acting in the capacity of judge and jury and passing the sentence: "Down the canyon for you," meaning thereby that the miner so addressed was discharged and ordered to leave the camp, upon miners who had incurred the enmity of the superintendent or pit boss for having complained of a real grievance or for other cause. . . .

Having established their control of public officials and successfully prevented the organization of their employees, the companies found little difficulty in disregarding the laws that had been enacted by the state legislature to protect the interests of the miners. As in other instances that have come to the attention of the Commission, laws proved almost if not quite worthless when not supported by a strong and aggressive organization of the men in whose interests they were enacted. . . .

For eleven years after the people of the State had ordered the enactment of an eight-hour law, the companies successfully defied the popular will and succeeded in blocking the enforcement of effective legislation. When at last they granted the eight-hour day, in March, 1913, we have the word of Mr. Bowers that it was not respect for this popular will, but the desire to defeat unionization, that actuated them. No more convincing evidence could be obtained of the necessity for economic organization by the workers to vitalize and make effective their political power.

Of all the specific grievances of the miners growing out of economic and political domination by the employers, one of the most serious was the denial of checkweighmen at the mine scales and the consequent lack of adequate assurance that the miners were being paid for all the coal they mined. There was not only a lack of such assurance; there was actual and deliberate cheating of miners by many of the coal operators, if we may take the word of Mr. Bowers, chief executive of the Colorado Fuel & Iron Company. This uncertainty and suspicion as to whether or not they were being paid in full for the coal mined contributed as much to the sense of injustice and acute dissatisfaction under which the miners labored as any other specific abuse. The testimony of striking miners before the Congressional Committee shows that they firmly believed themselves to have been the victims of petty cheating and larceny practiced by the companies, and that they felt helpless to protest. Yet by a state law enacted in 1897 the miners were given a right to employ checkweighmen whenever they desired to do so. . . .

Here again the legal rights of the miners proved worthless in the absence of a strong union. In denying them the union, the companies denied them the machinery with which to select a checkweighman in whose independence they could place their confidence. Fifty or one hundred or five hundred disorganized men, with half a dozen nationalities represented among them, could hardly be expected to meet together and act in harmony on the selection of a man to check the weights of their coal, when in all other respects they were forced to act individually, and were denied the training in collective action which only the union can give. . . .

Regarding the strikers' demand for the right to trade where they pleased, the testimony shows that mine employees, particularly in closed camps, risked the displeasure of the local officials, and the possibility of discharge, if they did not trade at the company stores. These stores were operated through subsidiary companies, all of the stock of which was owned by the mining companies. They earned very large profits. President Welborn of the Colorado Fuel & Iron Company testified that the stores of that company earned more than 20 per cent on a capital of $700,000. In about half the camps of this company the stores had no competition. Mr. Osgood of the Victor-American Company testified that the stores of his company earned 20 per cent. . . .

In at least half of the mining camps the company stores had no competition, except itinerant hucksters, and in the buying of his food and supplies, the miner was at the mercy of the company. In towns fifteen, twenty and thirty years old, this absence of competition can only be ascribed to the refusal of the companies to sell land for homes or other purposes, and this refusal in turn appears to have been actuated by a desire to monopolize the merchandising as well as every other activity of the community. . . .

Coupled with the strikers' demand for freedom to trade was the demand that they be allowed to choose their own boarding place and their own doctor. Considered as parts of the feudalistic system, company boarding houses, and company doctors contributed their share to a situation that altogether was intolerable to freemen. Both are institutions that could be maintained on a basis satisfactory to the miners if a strong union existed and the employees could effectively voice grievances as to this as well as to other features of company management. . . .

It remains to discuss, among the purposes for which political domination was used, the companies' control over coroners, sheriffs, and juries whose duties included the investigation of personal injury cases or the awarding of damages for these injuries.

Reports of the State Inspector of Coal Mines of Colorado show that prior to 1909 the number of deaths in the coal mining industry have been nearly two to one for the United States as [a] whole and from 1909 to 1913, about three and one-third to one. . . .

Rev. Mr. Gaddis gives the death roll of the Colorado Fuel & Iron Co., in major explosions, omitting accidents in which only one or two lives were lost, as follows: April 2, 1906, [at] Quartro, 19 killed; January 23, 1907, at Primero, 22 killed; May 5, 1907, at Engleville, 5 killed; January 31, 1910, at Primero, 76 killed; October 8, 1910, at Starkville, 56 killed. Total, 178 killed in five years. . . .

The testimony shows that personal injur[y] suits against the companies are practically unknown, and that injured miners or the widows and children of killed miners are forced to accept whatever compensation the attorneys and other agents of the corporations see fit to give them. . . .

Mr. McQuarrie [former undersheriff of Huerfano County] said he knew of no case where the company was held responsible for negligence by a coroner's jury, and that as a rule the juries found that the victim met his death by his own carelessness.

Mr. J. H. Patterson, a deputy clerk [in the county of] Walsenburg, presented to the Commission in Denver a certified copy of the record of the last ninety verdicts rendered by coroners' juries in Huerfano county. These ninety verdicts recorded the deaths of 109 persons, of whom 82 did not speak English. In only one verdict of the 90 was the mine management held at fault, and 85 of them, testified Mr. Patterson, bore the language "his own negligence," or, "his own carelessness." . . .

The use of political control to deny justice to injured workmen and the families of employees killed or maimed in accidents must be regarded as the most dastardly of all the unsocial and criminal practices that caused the strike.

19

OFFICE OF JOHN D. ROCKEFELLER JR. AND L. M. BOWERS

Correspondence on the Colorado Fuel and Iron Company and the Colorado Strike

1913

One of the wealthiest Americans of his day, John D. Rockefeller Jr. was the son of the founder of Standard Oil and helped run the family's corporate and philanthropic interests. Because the powerful Rockefeller family was a major stockholder in Colorado Fuel and Iron (CFI), the Commission on Industrial Relations closely scrutinized the younger Rockefeller's role in the strike. During the investigation, the commission subpoenaed all correspondence between his New York office (written by Rockefeller or his chief assistant, Starr Murphy) and CFI's executive chairman in Denver, L. M. Bowers. These letters provide a frank view of the company's attitudes toward the strike, the United Mine Workers and its demands, and the intervention of state and federal officials. In particular, they detail CFI's efforts to enlist Colorado banks and businesses to convince Governor Elias Ammons to deploy National Guard troops to the strike zone and escort strikebreakers into the mines. The correspondence also sheds light on the relationship between CFI and Rockefeller and the latter's knowledge of and position on the labor question. The Commission on Industrial Relations would later stress the differences between this correspondence and Rockefeller's earlier testimony before the commission, in which he had claimed that CFI policy on the strike "was reached without any consultation or communication with me."[1]

SEPTEMBER 19, 1913.

Dear Mr. Murphy:

... I will state as briefly as possible the demands of the organizers and agitators of the United Mine Workers of America and our relation at the present time in connection therewith.

[1] U.S. Commission on Industrial Relations, *Final Report and Testimony* (Washington, D.C., 1916), 8: 7764–65.

From U.S. Commission on Industrial Relations, *Final Report and Testimony* (Washington, D.C., 1916), 9: 8414–22, 8427.

We have spent a great deal of time and studied with a good deal of care all the questions in connection with labor unions among miners and men employed by industrial corporations during the past two or three years, anticipating in time having to meet the demands of union labor. . . .

We studied the eight-hour problem, which we knew would come up in the form of bills in the legislature and would be pushed through by agitators on the ground who were backing them, so we anticipated these matters and experimented with eight-hour labor. . . . Generally speaking, we found that working our mines eight hours saved us in overhead expenses and in other ways enough to offset any loss that might come from an 8 instead of a 9 or 10 hour day in many of our mines. After this had been thoroughly settled in our minds we established an eight-hour day for all coal miners, complying with the union rules in that respect, but operating as nonunion mines. . . .

Another matter was the weighmen[2] employed at the mines. For several years our company has raised no objection but has requested our miners to select their own weighmen, as is done in eastern mines where union labor is employed. This weighman has to be paid by a small assessment against each miner. Trifling though it is, our men would perhaps employ a weighman for a month, and then becoming satisfied that our own weighman was giving them correct weights, they invariably refused to continue the one selected by them. As our miners shift more or less and new men are coming all the while, about a year ago Mr. Welborn and the writer were discussing these questions, because one or two competitive companies . . . were cheating their miners by false weights, which some newspapers had taken up, and we agreed to post circulars at all our mines stating that we had always encouraged miners to employ their own weighmen, which our old employees were all familiar with, but for the benefit of newcomers we posted the notice to advise them that they were welcome to and urged to select their own weighmen. So far as I know not a single man was selected.

Another question was the accusation that miners were forced to trade at the company stores. In order to settle this we had our storekeepers and all interested say to our employees that they were welcome to trade at our stores or go anywhere they wished, as the money was their own; . . . they were perfectly free to trade where they pleased, and no man's standing would be changed if he saw fit not to trade with us. . . . Since the agitators have been in the State, we have had men

[2]Checkweighmen.

make a careful canvass of our camps and we have yet to find a single case of dissatisfaction on this account.

The above covers every demand being made now by the agitators, with the exception of recognition of the union and a trumped-up demand of a 10 per cent advance, which is entirely buncombe,[3] as our scales of wages practically conform to those of other bituminous-coal sections, and the average wages of our men are higher than in any other soft-coal mining section we know of. This is included in their demand to fool the public and to inspire our miners to unite with the union.

The main question, and, in fact, the only matter up between the United Mine Workers of America and the Colorado Fuel & Iron Co., is recognition of the union, which we flatly refuse to do, or even meet with these agitators to discuss or take up this question directly or indirectly.

Northern Colorado has had a strike for three and a half years. The companies were handicapped for a year or more, but have whipped the organization and are operating to full capacity without any serious difficulty as nonunion mines. They formerly employed union miners, whose rules became so oppressive that the operators were compelled to rid themselves of union dictation.

I will not undertake to enumerate these objections to union labor here. They are many. One is the quality of the output under union domination, which is inferior. It is impossible to discharge incompetent labor without the matter being brought up for investigation by officials of the union, both in and out of the State, and numerous requirements that practically take away the mines from the control of the owners and operators and place them in the hands of these, in many cases, disreputable agitators, socialists, and anarchists.

In canvassing our numerous mines we find practically all of our miners opposed to a strike or any disturbance in the relations existing between the company and themselves, including possibly 5 or 10 per cent who are inactive members of unions. These labor agitators have caused to be circulated throughout the United States false statements, which Mr. Welborn says are 100 percent lies. In other words, they claim that all the things above enumerated, which have been put in operation by our company without demands or solicitation, are unobserved in southern Colorado. While they may be able to find a few little operators who are unable to meet all the requirements and who are not doing as well for their miners as we are, they make no distinction and give the impression broadcast that all the coal mines of southern Colorado,

---

[3] Bunkum; nonsense.

including our own, are guilty of violating all of these rules which the unions have been able to secure in many sections of the country. So far as we are concerned, every single word is false. We have the good will of our men, and they are perfectly satisfied. Not more than 10 per cent belong to unions, and these are old miners who have belonged to unions in the Eastern States for many years and retain their membership as a matter of sentiment, rather than of protection.

It is difficult to tell what the outcome of the threatened strike will be. . . . Though we hope to be able to keep a large number of our men, many of those who do go out will, after a few days when they find we are able to protect them, return to their work. The strike is called for the 23d. . . .

This covers practically the whole matter, so far as the Colorado Fuel & Iron Co. is concerned. . . .

Yours, very truly,

L. M. Bowers

SEPTEMBER 29, 1913.

Dear Mr. Rockefeller:

Mr. Welborn and the writer have read your letter of the 24th, and we appreciate your very kind remarks in regard to our management of the affairs of the C. F. & I. Co. . . .

In southern Colorado, where we are so largely interested, from 40 to 60 per cent of the miners have quit work, but it is safe to say that out of an estimate of 8,000 men who are out, 7,000 of them have quit from fear of the Black Hand and similar organizations, who, through letters or face to face, threaten to kill the men, do violence to their wives and daughters, and practice all of the hellish villainy that these creatures possess. One of our marshals, who was one of the best men in our employ, was deliberately shot by Greeks when he undertook to stop them from tearing down a bridge. A bus carrying a few men was held up by 25 or more striking miners and the occupants ordered to leave the camp. These men happened not to be miners, but employees of railroads, which probably saved them from a severe beating up when that fact was discovered.

Hayes, vice president of the United Mine Workers of America, together with representatives here in this State, are the principal mischief makers. They have been able to load some newspapers with their lying statements and are permitted to gather gangs and crowds together in the streets, making speeches that would scarcely be permitted in any European country. . . .

Mr. Ethelbert Stewart, who called at your office, is in the State and is surrounded by and associated with Hayes, Brake, Lawson,[1] and other men of that stamp who are at the bottom of this strike. Mr. Stewart spent part of one afternoon with me, going over every point raised by these agitators, and he confessed that the Colorado Fuel & Iron Co. were meeting every requirement of organized labor in any bituminous coal-mining section of this country. . . .

We have given particular attention, as stated in my letter to Mr. Murphy, to the well-being of our men, as it has been one of the foremost things that I have always taken up in all of the corporations I have been connected with; and as I told your father in the first interview that we ever had, nearly 20 years ago, I would flatly refuse to be connected with any business enterprise where I would be handicapped in uplifting and benefiting mankind, especially those in our employ. This I told to Mr. Stewart, and suggested that he investigate every corporation with which I have been connected for the last 25 years or more, and see if he could find a place where this has not been one of the matters that has received my most careful consideration. He said he did not question this statement and that he had heard of it before coming here. I said that, in view of this, together with the fact that not more than 5 or 6 per cent of our men were members of unions after all the effort that had been made here for two or three years, we flatly refused to force 8,000 or 10,000 men to join the union and we be the collectors of $20,000 or $30,000 a month from our employees' wages and forward this amount to headquarters to be spent by the agitators in stirring up strife and discord and inevitable revolution in this country. He was told that we would work such mines as we could protect and close the others. . . .

Yours, very truly,

L. M. Bowers.

NEW YORK, OCTOBER 6, 1913.

Dear Mr. Bowers:

I have your letter of September 29, with reference to the coal strike in southern Colorado. . . .

---

[1]Stewart was a Bureau of Labor Statistics official dispatched by President Woodrow Wilson to mediate the strike. Edwin V. Brake was deputy state labor commissioner in Colorado. John Lawson was a United Mine Workers leader.

. . . We feel that what you have done is right and fair and that the position which you have taken in regard to the unionizing of the mines is in the interest of the employees of the company. Whatever the outcome may be, we will stand by you to the end.

Very truly,

John D. Rockefeller, Jr.

NOVEMBER 18, 1913.

Dear Mr. Rockefeller:
. . . You will be interested to know that we have been able to secure the cooperation of all the bankers of the city, who have had three or four interviews with our little cowboy governor, agreeing to back the State and lend it all the funds necessary to maintain the militia and afford ample protection so that our miners could return to work, or give protection to men who are anxious to come up here from Texas, New Mexico, and Kansas, together with some from States farther east. Besides the bankers, the chamber of commerce, the real estate exchange, together with a great many of the best business men, have been urging the Governor to take steps to drive these vicious agitators out of the State. Another mighty power has been rounded up in behalf of the operators by the gathering together of fourteen of the editors of the most important newspapers in Denver, Pueblo, Trinidad, Walsenburg, Colorado Springs, and other of the larger places in the State. They passed resolutions demanding that the governor bring this strike to an end, as they found, upon most careful examination, that the real issue was the demand for recognition of the union, which they told the governor would never be conceded by the operators as 90 per cent of the miners themselves were non-union men, and therefore that issue should be dropped. . . .

There probably has never been such pressure brought to bear upon any governor of this State by the strongest men in it as has been brought to bear upon Gov. Ammons. . . .

Yours, very truly,

L. M. Bowers.

DECEMBER 22, 1913.

Dear Mr. Rockefeller:
If the governor had acted on September 23 as he has been forced to act during the past few weeks [providing armed National Guard

escorts for the strikebreakers], the strike would have never existed 10 days.

... He was glove in hand with the labor leaders and is to-day, but the big men of affairs have helped the operators in whipping the agitators, including the governor.

... The inclosed is a sample of the resolutions being sent to him, besides any number of personal letters.

By the number of miners we are getting in from South and East, we will have all we can work in a week or so. . . .

I have never known such widespread approval by all classes of business men as we are getting in our fight for the "open shop."

We are paying the 4 per cent dividend for the last half of the current year on the preferred stock. . . .

Yours, very truly,

L. M. Bowers.

20

UNITED MINE WORKERS OF AMERICA

Governor Elias M. Ammons, Spineless Tool of the Coal Operators (Cartoon)

1914

This cartoon, which appeared in a 1914 report on the Ludlow Massacre issued by the United Mine Workers of America (UMWA), offers a biting commentary on the relationship between Colorado governor Elias Ammons and the state's coal operators, particularly John D. Rockefeller Jr., pictured in the upper left corner. The image plays on then common stereotypes of corporate plutocrats while offering a stark rebuff to Rockefeller's public claims that he had little or nothing to do with the Colorado strike.

From Walter H. Fink, District 15 UMWA, "The Ludlow Massacre," in *Massacre at Ludlow: Four Reports*, ed. Leon Stein and Philip Taft (New York: Arno Press, 1971), 64.

GOVERNOR ELIAS M. AMMONS, SPINELESS TOOL OF THE
COAL OPERATORS

21

COLORADO STATE FEDERATION OF LABOR

Militarism in Colorado

1914

The arrival of the Colorado National Guard in late October 1913 did little to stem the rising tide of violence in the strike zone. Before long, relations between strikers and soldiers turned hostile, generating further resentments and conflict on both sides. In December, the Colorado State Federation of Labor appealed to the governor, charging the Colorado National Guard with brutality, civil rights abuses, and other misconduct. At the suggestion of the governor, the federation appointed a committee, headed by Professor James Brewster of the University of Colorado Law School, to investigate the misconduct charges. The committee interviewed 163 witnesses, collected 760 pages of testimony, and issued "Militarism in Colorado," a thirteen-page report submitted to the governor in January 1914. Because General John Chase, commander of the National Guard troops, did not permit the committee to interview any soldiers, the report mainly reflects the viewpoints of the strikers and their sympathizers in the community.

We began taking testimony on December 23 and on the 24th met General Chase. . . .

That General Chase is laboring under a grave misapprehension as to his true functions in the strike district was disclosed to us during this meeting with him. He spoke of the existence of a "state of war" as justifying his total disregard of the constitution; he referred grandly to the duties and honor of "the soldier" and to "the soldier's" patient endurance of criticism without a murmur. Some of the officers and men in other camps, having a more correct conception of their duties, are not ashamed to say that they all are simply policemen, but this

---

From Colorado State Federation of Labor, "Militarism in Colorado: Report of the Committee Appointed at the Suggestion of the Governor of Colorado to Investigate the Conduct of the Colorado National Guard during the Coal Strike of 1913–1914" (Denver, 1914), 4, 6–7, 9–11. Page references to testimony have been deleted.

assumption of General Chase and some of his immediate advisers that they are soldiers engaged in war accounts for most of the errors of the militia—errors which range all the way from pitiful, puerile blunders to the grossest atrocities. . . .

There has been neither war, invasion nor insurrection. Much, however, has been done and is daily being done by the militia to incite striking miners to fight. Some such things are done merely from a lack of ordinary common sense, but other things are being done seemingly for no other purpose than to cause trouble. There has been as yet no such condition of affairs as would warrant the substitution of one man's will for the constitution and laws of the state—even could such a condition ever exist. Nevertheless, "The Military District of Colorado" has been established without legal authority, which "district" has the same territorial limits as the state of Colorado, and within this "district" General Chase is dictator. So far as he is concerned, the state's constitution and statutes are in abeyance.

One would expect that, accompanying military magnificence so great and soldier's honor so noble, there would be found a reasonable degree of discipline and a deportment conforming somewhat to that of modern armies of civilized nations, but we had hardly reached Trinidad before we heard on all sides of the scandalous behavior of the militiamen in saloons, cafes, on the streets, and in houses of ill repute, since their arrival nearly two months before. . . .

The character of some of this unsoldierlike conduct is illustrated by the testimony of Rev. James McDonald, as to the loose women throwing their arms about militiamen on the streets of Aguilar, in broad daylight; by militiamen "rushing the can"[1] in the town hall of Aguilar; by drunkenness while on sentry duty, and by their actions in saloons at many places. Drunken militiamen have frightened children; have threatened to shoot a boy of twelve; have stopped persons going about their business on the streets; have insulted waitresses. Our chief concern with this sort of thing is that it shows the kind of men who form part of the organized militia, and emphasizes the lack of discipline which characterizes a large portion of the body now in the field. The conduct of many of the men can be explained only by the fact that some companies have been recruited from the very scum of humanity, and have received as members former mine guards and private detectives, who have their own special grudges against the miners. . . .

---

[1]Carrying beer in a can or pail from a saloon to another location.

When citizens have protested to General Chase concerning the immoral conduct of the militia, his answer has been to call such accusations lies, and loftily to refer to such stories as "besmirching the soldier's uniform." Robberies and holdups by militiamen he disposes of in the same way; but the instances of this sort of valorous conduct are far too numerous, too varied in circumstances and scattered over too wide a territory to be so simply gotten rid of. They range from a forced loan of twenty-five cents; or whiskey "for the captain"; or a compulsory gift of three dollars; or whiskey, gin, cigars and champagne; or a ton of coal, to the downright robbery of $300, and other considerable sums of money, with watches and other small pieces of property. . . .

The pretense that the leaders of the militia have been impartial is absurd. A villainous mine guard may walk the streets, with his hand ready on his half-concealed gun in his coat pocket, and assault a union boy at noonday—as one guard did on Sunday, January 4th, at Walsenburg, while this committee was there—without interference from the militia, whereas a union man will be arrested and compelled by militiamen to work on a coal company ditch two days for being drunk when as a fact, drunkenness among the militia is more common than it is among the strikers. Other union men and boys have been arrested without being guilty of even drunkenness, and have been compelled by the militia to work at hauling coal or clearing snow for as long as five days.[2] The thirteenth amendment to the federal constitution is as unknown to the militia as are other laws.

The militia have tried to persuade strikers to go back to work, in some instances threatening and abusing them at the same time; a major offers to release an arrested union man if he will work in the mine; mine guards have given orders to militiamen as to the arrest and release of strikers, just as the coal company's attorney appears to have advised Chase and [Major Edward] Boughton, and a mine superintendent to have given orders to militiamen as to who should travel a public road, or whether a military pass should be cancelled; militiamen were present when a Polish ex-soldier, arriving as a strikebreaker, was offered by a mine superintendent a deputy's star, a six-shooter and a rifle—"an easy job and good pay"—provided he could shoot.

[2]This unpaid labor by prisoners is equated with slavery, prohibited under the Thirteenth Amendment.

On December 30th one negro shot another at the Ludlow tent colony of strikers during a quarrel. Similar events occur in Denver several times a month; but here was proof that there were arms at Ludlow, so the next day the camp was surrounded by cavalry, the coal operators' rapid-fire machine gun was trained on the women and children, and the tents were searched. In the 275 tents there were found, counting old and useless guns and pistols, about fifty pieces of arms. Before condemning as murderers the possessors of these arms, let the impartial General Chase explain why he has allowed shipments of arms in large quantities to be made to the mines. Why may mine superintendents equip with firearms mine guards and ex-soldiers of foreign armies and instruct them to shoot to kill? Is the constitutional right of every one "to keep and bear arms in defense of his home, person or property" intended solely for the protection of the operators' property? Are the track, the tipple and the tank more precious than the lives and liberties of men? If so, let us no longer pretend that this is a country for free men; let us openly announce that the dictator's will is our law, and let us blow the constitution to shreds at the mouth of the mine owner's machine gun.

The military authorities, while professing intense fairness, have allowed the coal operators to import strike-breakers, in direct violation of the state law passed in 1911 forbidding the importation of laborers into this state by means of false representation or false advertisement. It is a proven fact that the majority of workmen enticed into the mines since the inauguration of this strike have been deceived as to the existence of a strike, or rate of pay, or both. In spite of this open and flagrant violation of the plain letter and spirit of the statute the militia have met the trains bearing these deceived workmen, barring from the vicinity of the depots all persons who might inform these poor dupes of their rights under the law, and have escorted them to the coal camps, co-operating with the coal company guards in keeping them there whether they wished to leave or not. . . .

On December 31 we called your attention, in the following telegram from Trinidad, to a specific instance of [Lieutenant Karl] Linderfelt's cruelty which had come under our immediate notice:

"We did not expect to report to you until we had completed the taking of testimony at all camps, but in our judgment the following serious matters should be reported to you at once: Lieut. E. K. Linderfelt, of the cavalry stationed at Berwind, last night at Ludlow brutally assaulted an inoffensive boy in the public railroad station, using the vilest language at the same time. He also assaulted and tried to provoke to violence Louis Tikas, head man of the Ludlow strikers' colony, and arrested him unjustifiably. Today in the presence of one of our number he grossly abused a young man in no way connected with the strike, saying, among other things, 'I am Jesus Christ, and my men on horses are Jesus Christs, and we must be obeyed'; also making threats against the strikers in foulest language. He rages violently upon little or no provocation, and is wholly an unfit man to bear arms and command men, as he has no control over himself. We have reason to believe that it is his deliberate purpose to provoke the strikers to bloodshed. In the interest of peace and justice, we ask immediate action in his case." Signed by all the committee.

The testimony of ten different persons (seven of whom have no connection with the miners' union) sustaining these charges may be found on the accompanying pages. Part of Linderfelt's unreasoning rage was due to his assumption, without investigation, that a cavalryman's fall had been caused by a wire purposely stretched across the road, whereas the simple fact was that he had driven off the road and too near a post from which dangled a wire that tripped his horse. Linderfelt was quite like some of his superiors in brutally punishing first and investigating afterwards. Has Linderfelt been dishonorably discharged?

Every decent member of the militia who knows Louis Tikas—practically the head man of the Ludlow colony of strikers—will testify that he is an admirable man for the place he fills; that he is fair, and that he will assist the militia in every proper way in policing the neighborhood, yet it is this man whom Linderfelt tries to provoke in order that the other members of the colony will be aroused out of sympathy, and it is this man whom Linderfelt is reported to have threatened to kill on the slightest provocation. Linderfelt's extreme anti-union zeal and his brutal conduct justify belief in the common rumor that he is a "Baldwin" detective. Tikas was one of those arrested without warrant, held in prison for weeks, and discharged without any legal accusation. Others unreasonably arrested, held and discharged in the same manner, are: Gonzales, 53 days; King, 19 days; Zeni, 44 days; Thiros, 22 days; Titsworth, 12 days; Phillippi, 18 days; Zaginis, 14 days; Markas, 25 days; Barrego, 5 days, and others, like the railroad men, and the boys and men who were made to work for the militia to whom we have before referred.

To the foregoing instances of the militiamen's cruelties to men (which are a part only of what the testimony shows), must be added their insults and indignities to women—a few only of which have been mentioned. A young Slavic widow of nineteen, soon to become a mother, is dragged through an alley at night—a militiaman's hand over her mouth to smother her screams—till at length she faints and falls unconscious. Eight or ten men seized her and a woman with her as they were getting coal in the alley, and they were thus seized and dragged because these militiamen heard a shot in the neighborhood. Since it is a pastime of the militia to shoot their guns as playthings and discharge them indiscriminately, this incident would be ludicrous were it not so pathetically tragic. Unprotected women have been roused from sleep by militiamen attempting to enter their homes at night. Young girls have been grossly insulted by militiamen on the public street, and their protesting father laughed at. A modest young wife has her baby taken from her while she is threatened with grossest abuse by the militiamen. Restaurant waitresses are so insulted by militiamen that they will not wait upon them. . . .

. . . We ask, sir, your solemn consideration of this question: How much longer will workingmen continue to follow the Stars and Stripes when they repeatedly see the principles for which the Stars and Stripes have stood contemptuously disregarded by those in whose hands for a time lies might without right?

The usurpation of authority by the military is a matter of grave moment to every one. The force that today is directed against those whom some in their ignorance and short-sightedness regard as inferior beings may tomorrow be turned against these same superior persons and their friends. . . .

> Respectfully submitted,
> (Signed) JOHN R. LAWSON,
> ELI M. GROSS,
> JAMES H. BREWSTER,
> FRANK T. MINER,
> JAMES KIRWAN,
> Committee.

22

MOTHER JONES

In Rockefeller's Prisons

1925

Mary Harris Jones, known as "Mother Jones," was a legendary activist and orator in the Colorado coal strike of 1913–1914. Born into a Catholic laboring family in Cork, Ireland, in 1837, Harris grew up among the hardships and suffering of the Irish potato famine. In the early 1850s, she immigrated to Canada with her family and later worked as a schoolteacher and dressmaker in the United States. She moved to Memphis, Tennessee, in 1860, where she married an iron molder and union activist named George Jones and gave birth to four children. In the summer of 1867, a yellow fever epidemic engulfed the city, killing Mary's husband and children and leaving her a widow at age thirty. Tragedy seemed to follow her as she moved to Chicago to resume work as a dressmaker. A few years later, she and thousands of other residents lost their homes and livelihoods to the Great Chicago Fire of 1871.

Surviving such tragedies, Jones developed a keen awareness of the plight of the working poor and joined the Knights of Labor, one of the first national labor organizations. In the 1890s, Jones embarked on an itinerant career as a radical labor organizer that took her to countless strikes and labor conflicts over the next thirty years. It was during this time that she cast herself as "Mother Jones," a white-haired, grandmotherly figure who championed the rights of the downtrodden. She was particularly active in the United Mine Workers, which hired her as a paid organizer and sent her to strike zones in Pennsylvania, West Virginia, and Colorado. Her oratorical skills were formidable. She often kept audiences in rapt attention for hours, and she became known as "the miners' angel." She also worked hard to organize community-wide strike support by leading protest parades of women and children and organizing miners' wives to walk the picket line. Employers and local authorities

From Mother Jones, *The Autobiography of Mother Jones* (1925; repr., Chicago: Charles H. Kerr, 1976), 178–88, 190–91.

dreaded her arrival, and she was imprisoned and expelled from strike
zones on numerous occasions.

Mother Jones was seventy-six years old when her fiery speech to miners
in Trinidad helped launch the Colorado coal strike in September 1913.
In the coming months, she was jailed and sent away from the coalfields
three times. In her autobiography, she describes how she snuck back into
the strike zone in January 1914 and was later arrested and imprisoned
by the military.

I was in Washington, D.C., at the time of the great coal strike against
the Rockefeller holdings in southern Colorado. . . .

One day I read in the newspaper that Governor Ammons of
Colorado said that Mother Jones was not to be allowed to go into the
southern field where the strike was raging.

That night I took a train and went directly to Denver. I got a room
in the hotel where I usually stayed. I then went up to Union headquarters of the miners, after which I went to the station and bought my
ticket and sleeper to Trinidad in the southern field.

When I returned to the hotel, a man who had registered when I did,
came up to me and said, "Are you going to Trinidad, Mother Jones?"

"Of course," said I.

"Mother, I want to tell you that the governor has detectives at the
hotel and railway station watching you."

"Detectives don't bother me," I told him.

"There are two detectives in the lobby, one up in the gallery, and
two or three at the station, watching the gates to see who board the
trains south."

I thanked him for his information. That night I went an hour or so
before the coaches were brought into the station way down into the
railway yards where the coaches stood ready to be coupled to the
train. I went to the section house. There was an old section hand
there. He held up his lantern to see me.

"Oh, Mother Jones," he said, "and is it you that's walking the ties!"

"It's myself," said I, "but I'm not walking. I have a sleeper ticket for
the south and I want to know if the trains are made up yet. I want to
go aboard."

"Sit here," he said, "I'll go see. I don't know." I knew he understood
without any explaining why I was there.

"I wish you would tell the porter to come back with you," said I.

He went off, his light bobbing at his side. Pretty soon he returned with the porter.

"What you want, Mother?" says he.

"I want to know if the berths are made up yet?"

"Do you want to get on now, Mother?"

"Yes."

"Then yours is made up."

I showed him my tickets and he led me across the tracks.

"Mother," he said, "I know you now but later I might find it convenienter not to have the acquaintance."

"I understand," said I. "Now here's two dollars to give to the conductor. Tell him to let Mother Jones off before we get to the Santa Fe crossing. That will be early in the morning."

"I sure will," said he.

I got on board the sleeper in the yards and was asleep when the coaches pulled into the Denver station for passengers south. I was still asleep when the train pulled out of the depot.

Early in the morning the porter awakened me. "Mother," he said, "the conductor is going to stop the train for you. Be ready to hop."

When the train slowed down before we got to the crossing, the conductor came to help me off.

"Are you doing business, Mother?" said he.

"I am indeed," said I. "And did you stop the train just for me?"

"I certainly did!"

He waved to me as the train pulled away. "Goodbye, Mother."

It was very early and I walked into the little town of Trinidad and got breakfast. Down at the station a company of military were watching to see if I came into town. But no Mother Jones got off at the depot, and the company marched back to headquarters, which was just across the street from the hotel where I was staying.

I was in Trinidad three hours before they knew I was there. They telephoned the governor. They telephoned General Chase in charge of the militia. "Mother Jones is in Trinidad!" they said. . . .

My arrest was ordered.

A delegation of miners came to me. "Boys," I said, "they are going to arrest me but don't make any trouble. Just let them do it."

"Mother," said they, "we aren't going to let them arrest you!"

"Yes, you will. Let them carry on their game."

While we were sitting there talking, I heard footsteps tramping up the stairs.

"Here they come," said I and we sat quietly waiting.

The door opened. It was a company of militia.

"Did you come after me, boys?" said I. They looked embarrassed.

"Pack your valise and come," said the captain.

They marched me down stairs and put me in an automobile that was waiting at the door.

The miners had followed. One of them had tears rolling down his cheeks.

"Mother," he cried, "I wish I could go for you!"

We drove to the prison first, passing cavalry and infantry and gunmen, sent by the state to subdue the miners. Orders were given to drive me to the Sisters' Hospital, a portion of which had been turned into a military prison. They put me in a small room with white plastered walls, with a cot, a chair and a table, and for nine weeks I stayed in that one room, seeing no human beings but the silent military. One stood on either side of the cell door, two stood across the hall, one at the entrance to the hall, two at the elevator entrance on my floor, two on the ground floor elevator entrance.

Outside my window a guard walked up and down, up and down day and night, day and night, his bayonet flashing in the sun.

"Lads," said I to the two silent chaps at the door, "the great Standard Oil is certainly afraid of an old woman!"

They grinned.

My meals were sent to me by the sisters. They were not, of course, luxurious. In all those nine weeks I saw no one, received not a letter, a paper, a postal card. I saw only landscape and the bayonet flashing in the sun.

Finally, Mr. Hawkins, the attorney for the miners, was allowed to visit me. Then on Sunday, Colonel Davis came to me and said the governor wanted to see me in Denver.

The colonel and a subordinate came for me that night at nine o'clock. . . .

When we reached the Santa Fe crossing I was put aboard the train. I felt great relief, for the strike had only begun and I had much to do. I went to bed and slept till we arrived in Denver. Here I was met by a monster, called General Chase, whose veins run with ice water. He started to take me to Brown Palace Hotel. I asked him if he would permit me to go to a less aristocratic hotel, to the one I usually stopped at. He consented, telling me he would escort me to the governor at nine o'clock.

I was taken before the governor that morning. The governor said to me, "I am going to turn you free but you must not go back to the strike zone!"

"Governor," I said, "I am going back."

"I think you ought to take my advice," he said, "and do what I think you ought to do."

"Governor," said I, "if Washington took instructions from such as you, we would be under King George's descendants yet! If Lincoln took instructions from you, Grant would never have gone to Gettysburg. I think I had better not take your orders."

I stayed on a week in Denver. Then I got a ticket and sleeper for Trinidad. Across the aisle from me was Reno, Rockefeller's detective. Very early in the morning, soldiers awakened me.

"Get up," they said, "and get off at the next stop!"

I got up, of course, and with the soldiers I got off at Walsenburg, fifty miles from Trinidad. The engineer and the fireman left their train when they saw the soldiers putting me off.

"What are you going to do with that old woman?" they said. "We won't run the train till we know!"

The soldiers did not reply.

"Boys," I said, "go back on your engine. Some day it will be all right."

Tears came trickling down their cheeks, and when they wiped them away, there were long, black streaks on their faces.

I was put in the cellar under the courthouse. It was a cold, terrible place, without heat, damp and dark. I slept in my clothes by day, and at night I fought great sewer rats with a beer bottle. "If I were out of this dungeon," thought I, "I would be fighting the human sewer rats an[y]way!"

For twenty-six days I was held a military prisoner in that black hole. I would not give in. I would not leave the state. At any time, if I would do so, I could have my freedom. General Chase and his bandits thought that by keeping me in that cold cellar, I would catch the flu or pneumonia, and that would settle for them what to do with "old Mother Jones."

Colonel Berdiker, in charge of me, said, "Mother, I have never been placed in a position as painful as this. Won't you go to Denver and leave the strike field?"

"No, Colonel, I will not," said I.

The hours dragged underground. Day was perpetual twilight and night was deep night. I watched people's feet from my cellar window; miners' feet in old shoes; soldiers' feet, well shod in government leather; the shoes of women with the heels run down; the dilapidated shoes of children; barefooted boys. The children would scrooch down and wave to me but the soldiers shooed them off.

One morning when my hard bread and sloppy coffee were brought to me, Colonel Berdiker said to me, "Mother, don't eat that stuff!" After that he sent my breakfast to me—good, plain food. He was a man with a heart, who perhaps imagined his own mother imprisoned in a cellar with the sewer rats' union.

The colonel came to me one day and told me that my lawyers had obtained a habeas corpus for me and that I was to be released; that the military would give me a ticket to any place I desired.

"Colonel," said I, "I can accept nothing from men whose business it is to shoot down my class whenever they strike for decent wages. I prefer to walk."

"All right, Mother," said he, "goodbye!"

The operators were bringing in Mexicans to work as scabs in the mines. In this operation they were protected by the military all the way from the Mexican borders. They were brought in to the strike territory without knowing the conditions, promised enormous wages and easy work. They were packed in cattle cars, in charge of company gunmen, and if when arriving, they attempted to leave, they were shot. Hundreds of these poor fellows had been lured into the mines with promises of free land. When they got off the trains, they were driven like cattle into the mines by gunmen.

This was the method that broke the strike ten years previously. And now it was the scabs of a decade before who were striking—the docile, contract labor of Europe.

I was sent down to El Paso [Texas] to give the facts of the Colorado strike to the Mexicans who were herded together for the mines in that city. I held meetings, I addressed Mexican gatherings, I got the story over the border. I did everything in my power to prevent strike breakers going into the Rockefeller mines.

In January, 1914, I returned to Colorado. When I got off the train at Trinidad, the militia met me and ordered me back on the train. Nevertheless, I got off. . . .

The train for Denver pulled in. The military put me aboard it. When we reached Walsenburg, a delegation of miners met the train, singing a miner's song. They sang at the top of their lungs till the silent, old mountains seemed to prick up their ears. They swarmed into the train.

"God bless you, Mother!"

"God bless you, my boys!" . . .

Outside in the station stood the militia. One of them was a fiend. He went about swinging his gun, hitting the miners, and trying to prod them into a fight, hurling vile oaths at them. But the boys kept cool and I could hear them singing above the shriek of the whistle as the train pulled out of the depot and wound away through the hills.

From January on until the final brutal outrage—the burning of the tent colony in Ludlow—my ears wearied with the stories of brutality and suffering. My eyes ached with the misery I witnessed. My brain sickened with the knowledge of man's inhumanity to man. . . .

I sat through long nights with sobbing widows, watching the candles about the corpse of the husband burn down to their sockets.

"Get out and fight," I told those women. "Fight like hell till you go to Heaven!" That was the only way I knew to comfort them.

I nursed men back to sanity who were driven to despair. I solicited clothes for the ragged children, for the desperate mothers. I laid out the dead, the martyrs of the strike. I kept the men away from the saloons, whose licenses as well as those of the brothels, were held by the Rockefeller interests.

The miners armed, armed as it is permitted every American citizen to do in defense of his home, his family; as he is permitted to do against invasion. The smoke of armed battle rose from the arroyos and ravines of the Rocky Mountains.

No one listened. No one cared. The tickers in the offices of 26 Broadway sounded louder than the sobs of women and children. Men in the steam heated luxury of Broadway offices could not feel the stinging cold of Colorado hillsides where families lived in tents.

Then came Ludlow and the nation heard. Little children roasted alive make a front page story. Dying by inches of starvation and exposure does not.

23

ROCKY MOUNTAIN NEWS AND UNITED MINE WORKERS JOURNAL

The January 22 Riot

1914

Mother Jones was not the only woman to take a militant stand in support of the strike. In fact, her presence helped galvanize labor activism among strikers' wives and children. On January 22, 1914, a group of strikers' wives led a women's march to support the United Mine Workers and protest the imprisonment of Mother Jones. The National Guard, under the command of General John Chase, initially authorized the march but later attempted to stop the procession. A violent confrontation ensued in which several protesters and militiamen were injured. Newspapers gave dramatically different accounts of the incident, reflecting the political viewpoints of different segments of the community. The following two articles—one published in the Rocky Mountain News, *a Denver daily newspaper, the other in the* United Mine Workers Journal, *the official union publication—offer opposing views of the day's events and very different images of the protesters.*

FROM *ROCKY MOUNTAIN NEWS*

TRINIDAD, COLO., Jan. 22—Eighteen persons, including eight women, are under arrest and nearly a dozen are known to be suffering from injuries as the results of a serious street riot here this afternoon.

The militia, with drawn sabers and under the personal direction of Gen. John Chase, broke up a mob of strikers and strike sympathizers which was attempting to march to San Rafael hospital, where "Mother" Jones is held under military arrest.

Stones, bottles and bricks were hurled at the militiamen by a crowd of angry women who precipitated the outbreak when they were ordered to turn back by the soldiers.

From "Militia Sabers Slash Women in Riot at Trinidad," *Rocky Mountain News*, January 23, 1914; "Great Czar Fell!" *United Mine Workers Journal*, January 29, 1914.

Charge Crowd with Swords

Several soldiers, including Maj. H. M. Randolph, were assaulted, and not until the calvarymen, with drawn swords, had charged the crowd several times, was the mob dispersed. One soldier sustained a broken rib when his horse fell, and one of the rioters received a cut from a saber in the hands of a soldier. . . .

The riot followed a parade of wives and children of striking coal miners which had been carefully planned by the union leaders. Permission to carry out the plans had been granted by General Chase with the understanding that no effort would be made to march to the hospital. . . .

Following the riot, the women held a mass meeting and organized the "Women's Voting Association of Southern Colorado," the purpose of which is to defeat Governor Ammons and other state officers who have sanctioned the sending of the soldiers into the district, at the next election. Resolutions were indorsed condemning the actions of the governor and of General Chase.

FROM *UNITED MINE WORKERS JOURNAL*

TRINIDAD, COLO., Jan. 23—A craven general tumbled from his nag in a street of Trinidad Thursday, like Humpty-Dumpty from the wall!

In fifteen minutes there was turmoil, soldiers with swords were striking at fleeing women and children; all in the name of the sovereign State of Colorado.

For Gen. John Chase, having lost his poise on his horse, also lost his temper and cried, "Ride down the women!"

A throng of mothers and wives intent only on a mass meeting of sympathy for "Mother" Jones, had laughed at Chase's fall.

Then there was bloodshed!

The French revolution (its history written upon crimson pages) carries no more cowardly episode than the attack of the gutter gamin soldiery on a crowd of unarmed and unprotected women![1]

Women were ridden down by the soldiers' horses and struck by sabres, little children were endangered by the whirling hoofs of the cavalry horses, and all because "Czar" John Chase, adjutant-general of Colorado, after his fall, went mad when he heard the laughter of marching strikers.

---

[1] Refers to the Women's March on Versailles in 1789, when French women marched on the royal palace demanding bread.

"Czar" Chase, according to citizens who saw the whole affair, became so excited he tumbled from his mount at the start of the trouble.

The cavalry charge was made, Chase explained, because the women, wives, mothers and sisters of striking coal miners were prepared to march to San Rafael hospital, where 82-year-old "Mother" Jones has been a military prisoner for nearly two weeks.

The truth is, according to union officials and citizens here, that the line of march to be followed by the women had been explained to Chase; that he had agreed to it, and that he had then ordered soldiers stationed near the post office, where he knew the parade must pass.

When the parade approached there were nearly a thousand women and children in line. They had come to Trinidad from all over the strike district. Many of the women were mothers with babies in their arms. The children were dressed in their shabby best clothes, as for a holiday.

A crowd of men, strikers and strike sympathizers, followed the marching women and children. The parade was peaceable until the cordon of cavalry, stretched across Main street near the post office, was reached. There were *about* a hundred of the soldiers with loaded rifles and drawn swords. At the head was "Czar" Chase.

"Don't advance another step!" the parading women and children were told. "You must turn back!"

But they kept steadily marching along the street, where, it is claimed, they had forewarned Chase they intended to go.

Then it was that Chase fell from his horse. He says the animal stumbled. A shout of laughter went up from the women, as they saw the dignified general unhorsed.

Chase rose, pallid with wrath.

"Charge those women if they come another foot," he is said to have called to his soldiers. . . .

Telling in vivid words they said the cowardly charge made by the militiamen Thursday upon a group of defenseless women and children on the streets of Trinidad, a sheaf of affidavits from paraders and spectators was received here Friday.

Every affidavit agrees that marching women had no intention of going to San Rafael hospital, that they were merely following an arranged line of march, and that the soldiers' attack was most unwarranted.

24

COLORADO ADJUTANT GENERAL

The Battle of Ludlow
1914

On April 20, 1914, about a week after Governor Ammons withdrew most of the National Guard troops from the strike zone, a deadly conflagration erupted at Ludlow, killing twenty people. In the wake of this tragedy, Governor Ammons directed the commander of the Colorado National Guard to appoint a special board of officers to investigate the events of April 20. Comprising Major Edward Boughton, Captain William Danks, and Captain Philip Van Cise, the board conducted an immediate investigation based on interviews with officers, soldiers, deputies, mine guards, prisoners, and local residents. Although the board attempted to solicit testimony from strikers and their families, the United Mine Workers objected to its closed proceedings, and the union's members declined to participate. The report thus recounts the events of that day from the military's perspective and sheds light on some of the soldiers' attitudes toward the immigrant strikers at Ludlow.

The Ludlow tent colony, by far the largest of all such colonies, housed a heterogeneous population of striking miners. The colony numbered hundreds of people, of whom only a few families were Americans. The rest were for the most part Greeks, Montenegrins, Bulgars, Servians, Italians, Mexicans, Tyroleans, Croatians, Austrians, Savoyards, and other aliens from the southern countries of Europe. These people had little in common either with the few Americans resident among them, or with one another. Each nationality had its own leader, customs and mode of life. We are credibly informed that within the colony twenty-two different tongues were spoken, unintelligible one to another. . . .

From Colorado Adjutant General, "Ludlow: Being the Report of the Special Board of Officers Appointed by the Governor of Colorado to Investigate and Determine the Facts with Reference to the Armed Conflict between the Colorado National Guard and Certain Persons Engaged in the Coal Mining Strike at Ludlow, Colorado, April 20, 1914" (Denver, 1914), 6–24.

The most forceful portion of the colonists were the Greeks. We do not know that they outnumbered the other nationalities in the colony, but we are positive that they dominated it. The will of the Greeks was the law of the colony. They were the most aggressive element, the fighting men; and they imposed their desires upon the rest. . . .

Living in the immediate vicinity of the colonist population just described were three distinct groups of men controlled by distinct feelings toward the strikers. In the first group were the non-union workmen in the mines of the adjacent canons [canyons]. These men were dwelling with their families in the villages about the mines where they were employed. Most of them were recent arrivals, coming in as strikebreakers to take the strikers' places in the mines. This class is not to be confused, as it has been, with the mine guards. . . .

These mine guards formed another distinct class. They are men whose employment is to guard the properties; they are not permanent residents of the mine communities like the non-union workmen, but have come with the strike and will depart with it. The mine guards are usually employed through a detective agency making a specialty of such work. The strikers' ill will toward this agency and the armed guards it furnishes antedates the present trouble and is born of a long series of conflicts in other fields and other states. During the weeks before the coming of the soldiers last fall these armed mine guards and the strikers fought many a battle, from all of which it has come to pass that the deadliest hatred exists between the strikers of the tent colonies and the mine guards of the coal camps.

The third class of men in this vicinity consists of the uniformed and armed National Guardsmen who have been on duty during this campaign. With an exception to be noted presently, this class has no feeling either of hatred or of fear toward the colonists, whose nearest neighbors they were. Throughout the campaign a friendly relationship was maintained between the two groups of tents. . . . The exception referred to is the company of mounted infantry occupying the sub-station at Cedar Hill in Berwind Canon, designated Company "B" and commanded for the greater part of the campaign by Lieutenant K. E. Linderfelt. This officer is an experienced soldier and an inexperienced sociologist. He is a veteran of five wars, but wholly tactless in his treatment of both mine guards and strikers. From the beginning of the campaign this militia organization and the strikers in the colony were in frequent petty conflicts with one another. They grew to dislike each other and to worry, harass and annoy one another. . . .

The tent colony population is almost wholly foreign and without conception of our government. A large percentage are unassimilable aliens to whom liberty means license, and among whom has lately been spread by those to whom they must look for guidance a dangerous doctrine of property. Rabid agitators had assured these people that when the soldiers left they were at liberty to take for their own, and by force of arms, the coal mines of their former employers. They have been sitting in their tents for weeks awaiting the departure of the soldiers and the day when they could seize what they have been told is theirs. When the troops were withdrawn elsewhere and this one unit left at Ludlow, many of the strikers believed that the men whom they saw in uniform were no longer members of the National Guard, but hired gunmen or mine guards who retained their uniforms for want of other clothing. They saw the hated mine guards return. They were told by their leaders, as they have always been, that the mine guards intended to attack their colony. The greed, fears and most brutal hatreds of the violent elements were thus aroused, and they began to prepare for battle. They laid in a store of arms, two or three at a time. They bought quantities of ammunition, they built military earthworks in concealed places, they dug pits beneath their tents in which they designed to put their women and children as a place of safety. . . . The Greeks in particular, who had deeply resented the searching of the colony and the taking of their arms by the soldiers, swore that their arms should never be taken from them again. . . . The colony was electrified; a spark only was needed to set off an explosion. The spark fell unwittingly on Monday, the 20th of April.

As is usual with such inevitable conflicts, the battle was unexpectedly precipitated and by a trifling incident. Two facts in this connection stand out very clearly. One is that the conflict was contemplated, prepared against, deliberately planned and intended by some of the strikers, and was feared and expected by the soldiers and inhabitants of the mining villages. The other fact, equally clear, is that neither side expected it to fall at the time or in the manner that it did. . . . We find from examination of the colonists themselves that talk of such an attack upon the soldiers, to be followed by a seizure of the mines, expulsion of the non-union workmen and vengeance upon the mine guards, had been rife in the colony for many days. . . .

. . . For weeks before the withdrawal of the troops it had been a settled belief that some day, when the military force should be weakened, the strikers would undertake to wipe out soldiers and civilian workmen alike. But on the morning of the Ludlow conflict the idea of battle was furthest from the minds of the few remaining troopers. Had such an attack been planned by the military, the soldiers would have occupied the commanding positions and delivered it at dawn instead of allowing those places to be occupied by the strikers with such force that it took all day to drive the colonists from them. . . .

Lieutenant Linderfelt . . . received a letter from some foreign woman, claiming that her husband was being detained against his will in the tent colony. This letter was sent to Major Hamrock at the tents near the colony.

A few soldiers are detailed to meet every train to see that the passengers getting on or off are not molested by the colonists. By this train detail Major Hamrock sent word to the Greek leader, Louis Tikas, who was also chief man of the colony, calling attention to the letter and demanding the release of the writer's husband. Tikas denied that any such man was in the colony. . . . For the first time Tikas flatly refused to come to the Major's camp. Thereupon the Major telephoned to the station at Cedar Hill, and told the Captain in charge that he might have need of him and his men to search the colony for a man held prisoner there. The Cedar Hill detachment was ordered to drill on the parade ground at Water Tank Hill. . . .

In the meantime Tikas telephoned to the Major that he would meet him at the railroad station, which is about equi-distant from the two sets of tents. After this conversation Major Hamrock telephoned again to Cedar Hill and directed the remaining soldiers to join their troop on the parade ground, and to bring with them the machine gun.

We find that after the train detail left, Tikas was surrounded by his Greeks in the colony; and that these Greeks were under the impression that the colony was about to be again searched for arms—a thing which they had vowed they would never again permit. The Greeks were vociferous and insistent upon giving battle to the soldiers at once if they should appear. Tikas did the best he could to dissuade and quiet them. It was then that he called Major Hamrock by telephone. . . . Tikas met at the station Major Hamrock and the woman who had written the letter and who complained that her husband was being held a prisoner in the colony. Tikas recognized this woman and then stated that he knew her husband, who had been in the colony on Saturday, but was no longer there.

During this conversation at the station the first detachment from Cedar Hill arrived on Water Tank Hill, and their officer, Lieutenant Lawrence, galloped down to the station and reported to Major Hamrock.

... Three women, who had been to the store near the station, returned excitedly to the colony, and called the attention of the Greeks to the arrival of the troopers on Water Tank Hill. ... The Greeks, confirmed in their belief and consumed with a suppressed thirst for battle, forgetting their promise to Tikas, seized their rifles and defiled from the colony across country ... to a railroad cut on the Colorado & Southeastern tracks, affording excellent cover for delivering a rifle fire on Water Tank Hill. These Greeks, as nearly as we could discover, were estimated variously to number from thirty-five to fifty men. ...

At the same time there left the colony a much larger number of men of other nationalities, armed with rifles, going northwest to the arroyo [gully]. ...

Lieutenant Lawrence, having reported to the Major, left to return to his detachment on Water Tank Hill. He had gone but a short way when he galloped back to the station and cried out: "My God, Major, look at these men; we are in for it," pointing toward the Greeks defiling toward the railroad cut. Tikas was the first to answer ... saying, "I will stop them," and, pulling out his handkerchief, ran toward the colony, waving to the Greeks to return. ... After the Lieutenant reached Water Tank Hill, and not before, the machine gun and remaining men from Cedar Hill arrived. Major Hamrock hurried from the station to his tents, and reported the conditions to General Chase in Denver. While returning to his camp the Major observed the women and children of the colony in large numbers running from the colony north to the shelter of the arroyo. ... The exodus of women and children was sufficient to account for all that were known to be in the colony. ...

As yet no shot of any kind had been fired. In expectation of just such an attack, a signal had been devised. Two crude bombs were made of sticks of dynamite, and it was understood that if the colonists attacked suddenly, so that there was not time to telephone the various villages in the canons, or the wires were cut, these bombs should be exploded as a warning. After telephoning to Denver, the Major caused these bombs to be set off, and so far as we can learn, this was the first explosion of the day. ...

... About the time the Greeks reached the cover of the railroad cut, the fire began. We are unable to state from which point the firing came first, except that it came from the strikers. ... The first of it was directed toward the soldiers' tents, but it must very soon have been directed generally against Water Tank Hill and the whole countryside between that point and the Hastings Canon. After the fire started, it was several minutes before the men on Water Tank Hill were directed to return it. ...

Shortly after the firing commenced, it became very general. On the strikers' side it proceeded from the railroad cut, from the tent colony and from the arroyo beyond it. It was returned from Water Tank Hill, from a row of steel cars in the vicinity of the soldiers' tents, and from houses and stores along the road between the colony and the northern canon. Lieutenant Lawrence and three men advanced from Water Tank Hill toward the Greek position in the railroad cut with a view to dislodge the men shooting from that cover. One of these men, Private Martin, was shot through the neck. . . . The strikers' fire proved insupportable, and the squad withdrew, helping Martin back with them. They were compelled to leave Martin under cover and return without him. As they retreated the strikers followed until under cover. . . . But it was not until the afternoon when Captain Carson arrived from Trinidad with reinforcements and another machine gun that they were able to drive the strikers back and reach the place where Martin lay. Just before dark this was accomplished and Martin was discovered dead and mutilated. He had been shot through the mouth, powder stains evidencing that the gun was held against his lips. His head had been caved in and his brains exuded on the ground. His arms had been broken. In such a way does the savage blood-lust of this Southern European peasantry find expression. In this connection we find also that without exception where dying or wounded adversaries, whether soldiers or civilians, had fallen into the hands of these barbarians they were tortured or mutilated. . . .

The recovery of Martin's body, thus mutilated, we find to have had the effect of exciting his comrades to a frenzy, which may account for some things that took place later near the tent colony itself. . . .

. . . Under the protection of the machine guns' fire, Captain Linderfelt, Captain Carson and Lieutenant K. E. Linderfelt were from this time able to advance steadily. They were accompanied by part of the Water Tank Hill detachment, the reinforcements from Trinidad in civilians' clothes, and some mine guards. Their fire was returned from their front all along the arroyo and from the tent colony itself. The men to the west between the colony and the canon were about this time likewise able to press closer to the arroyo and the tent colony. As both these forces approached the colony the heaviest fire seemed to come from the very tents themselves. . . . It was then that Major Hamrock tested his range with the machine guns on Water Tank Hill and sent them directly into the first tents of the colony itself, at the same time the strikers' fire drew a return from all combatants into the same tents. It was this concentrated fire upon the nearest tents in the southwest corner of the colony that set them on fire. . . . The women and children had been seen departing early in the morning, and it was impossible to believe that the strikers would draw the fire of their opponents from all sides into the colony if any women and children remained therein.

Shortly after the fire started the detonation of some high explosive like some giant powder or dynamite was both heard and seen. . . . As one tent caught after another, several other explosions occurred. During this time some of the men, having nearly reached the tent colony, heard the screams of women and called to men whom they saw firing from between the tents to get their women out. The only answer was the words, "You go to hell," spoken with a foreign accent and accompanied by a rain of shots. . . . Captain Carson, Lieutenant Linderfelt and other officers and men, made a dash in among the burning tents for the purpose of rescuing the women and children. At first they took several women from the tents, some of which were on fire and some not; then they discovered some subterranean pits beneath many of the tents and that some of them were stored with human occupants. The . . . women refused to accompany the soldiers and even fought against being taken away. They said afterwards that they believed the soldiers would kill them. They had to be dragged to places of safety. . . . We find that the work of rescuing these women and children, to the number of some twenty-five or thirty, by Lieutenant Linderfelt, Captain Carson, and the squads at their command, was under all the circumstances, truly heroic and must stand out boldly in contradistinction to the abandonment of the helpless women and children by their own people and the subsequent efforts to kill their rescuers, regardless of the safety of the rescued. It was supposed by the officers, after a thorough search of the colony, that all of the remaining women and children had been taken out. The event proved that one of the pits had been missed in the search. In this pit were subsequently discovered two women and eleven children, all dead. This chamber of death measured in feet $8 \times 6 \times 4\frac{1}{2}$. When found it was almost closed. The quantity of air contained in such a space we found could not have supported the life of these occupants for many hours. Their bodies, when found, bore heartrending evidences of their struggles to get out. . . . It is our belief that they died of suffocation hours before the tents caught fire. Among those taken out of the colony by the rescue parties was a man named Snyder and his family. The man carried in his arms the dead body of his little son. This boy had been shot in the forehead and was indeed the only person shot in the colony. . . .

... By this time, the time of the burning of the tents, the nondescript number of men had passed out of their officers' control, had ceased to be an army and had become a mob. ... Men and soldiers swarmed into the colony and deliberately assisted the conflagration by spreading the fire from tent to tent. Beyond a doubt it was seen to intentionally that the fire should destroy the whole of the colony. ... Men and soldiers seized and took from the tents whatever appealed to their fancy of the moment. In this way, clothes, bedding, articles of jewelry, bicycles, tools and utensils were taken from the tents and conveyed away. So deliberate was this burning and looting that we find that cans of oil found in the tents were poured upon them and the tents lit with matches. ...

... At this point [two soldiers] took a prisoner who proved to be Tikas, Louis the Greek. The men brought this prisoner back along the railroad to the Cross-Roads at the corner of the colony. ... Immediately between fifty and seventy-five men, uniformed soldiers, men of Troop "A" and mine guards, rushed to that point. ... Tikas was then turned over to the Lieutenant, his captors returning to their post. Some words ensued between the Lieutenant and Tikas over the responsibility for the day's doings. ... There were cries of "Lynch him" from the crowd. Someone ran into the tent colony and got a rope and threw it over a telegraph pole. Lieutenant Linderfelt had difficulty in restraining the crowd. He declared that there should be no lynching and turned the prisoner over to Sergeant Cullen, with instructions that he would hold the Sergeant responsible for Tikas' life. About this time two other prisoners were brought to the Cross-Roads. ... Filer, the secretary of the union, and an unknown whom we believe, however, to have been Frank Rubino. ... Lieutenant Linderfelt then went back along the tracks to the station. ... Shortly after the departure of Lieutenant Linderfelt, firing was resumed. The men returned to their places under cover of the railroad embankment and recommenced firing into the colony. The three prisoners ran through this fire toward the tents and were all shot before they reached them. Tikas was shot in the back, showing that he was killed from the soldiers' side. Filer, however, who got nearest to the tents, was shot in front, showing that he was killed from the strikers' side. ...

... We do not presume even to hint where the ultimate responsibility lies in the present strike. It may be that the coal operators or the union are wholly to blame for the conditions that have made such results possible; it may be that both sides are partly at fault. But the conditions having been brought about and being actually existent, whatever the cause, we feel that for their treason and rebellion against organized society, with the horrible consequences of anarchy that followed, certain union leaders must take the responsibility before man and God.

25

MARY THOMAS O'NEAL

Escape from Ludlow

1971

Many of the survivors of the Ludlow tragedy disagreed with the military board's version of the events of April 20, 1914 (Document 24). In interviews with the press and through their testimony to government investigators, civilian eyewitnesses gave chilling accounts of the military assault, the death of loved ones, the fate of prisoners, and harrowing escapes from the besieged tent camp. Among the strikers and their families, however, only Mary Thomas O'Neal left a detailed personal memoir of the strike and its bloody culmination at Ludlow. Born in Wales in 1887, she married a coal miner who later deserted the family and immigrated to the United States. Mary and her two children followed and eventually joined up with him in the coalfields of southern Colorado. Although the marriage quickly dissolved, O'Neal became a strong defender of the United Mine Workers and a resident of the Ludlow tent camp in 1913. In her autobiography, published in 1971, she gives a harrowing account of the April 20 attack and the desperate escape of several dozen women and children. Recorded more than fifty years later when she was eighty-four, her reminiscences are far removed from the events. Nevertheless, they offer a unique view of the Ludlow tragedy and highlight the importance of local networks of support for miners and their families.

It was around nine in the morning on Monday, April 20, 1914. My children and I had just finished our breakfast of oatmeal when we heard a

From Mary Thomas O'Neal, *Those Damn Foreigners* (Hollywood, Calif.: Minerva Book, 1971), 133–48.

terrific explosion. We ran outside, as did everyone else. "What was that?" we all asked each other.

Louie [Louis] Tikas' voice was heard over the megaphone. It sounded as if he were crying. "Now listen carefully. That was a warning bomb you just heard. The head guard has just told me that when the third bomb goes off this tent colony will be demolished. He told me to tell you, whom he calls "damn foreigners," that you and your families had better get out. . . . I beg of you to run for your lives. All miners with rifles go to the nearest hills to protect your tent homes, and men without rifles, run to the farther hills. Leave the women and children and go now. All women and children, RUN FOR YOUR LIVES. . . ."

Suddenly the prairie was covered with human beings running in all directions like ants. No one had time to get anything, save to pick up whatever food was on the table. We all ran as we were, some with babies on their backs, in whatever clothes we were wearing, leaving our tent homes behind us, snatching what we could take with us immediately, not even thinking through the clouds of panic. We were terrified. . . .

I dashed back to our tent to get the milk off the table. Tony [Gorsi, a neighbor in the camp] had no gun, so ran to the upper hills. I grabbed my girls and we started for the arroyo. Several of the women didn't understand English and shouted at me which way to go. I pointed toward it and beckoned them to follow me. . . .

. . . The frightened screeches and screams of all the women and children dashing over the prickly prairie were deafening. It was half a mile to the arroyo. On the way I came upon Margo, carrying her heavy ten month old baby, and dragging the one a year older. Her three year old boy clung to her skirts. She was wearing carpet slippers, her feet bleeding from the prickly brush. She could only go at a snail's pace.

I took the baby, and she carried the other, her boy pulling at her skirt and my two girls hanging onto mine. The women who didn't have babies, or had older children who could run, had already gone through the arroyo to get to Trinidad, wild with fright. . . . We weren't more than half way to the arroyo when the third bomb went off. Then the shooting started toward the tent colony . . . and at us. The guards couldn't help but see us out there in the brush, going as fast as we could, and they kept shooting at our heels, I suppose to hurry us on. My shoe came off. I stooped to put it back on, and a bullet hit me in the wrist, a mark I have to this day. At last Margo and our children and the women I'd beckoned to follow me with theirs, reached the arroyo, exhausted. . . .

There were eight dazed women and fifteen children now in the comparative safety of the arroyo, huddling together against its damp clay walls, with muddy water trickling along at our feet. We were hungry. None of us had time to grab anything to eat except what was on our tables. All we had was some stale bread, a little milk and some water.

Poor Margo's feet were killing her. I picked the brush stickers out of them which caused her such torture. . . .

We were there for hours, now out of food, milk and water. The shooting would cease for awhile, then start furiously again on both sides. When the gunfire would quiet down, some of us would climb the slick walls of the arroyo to see how much damage there might have been to our tent homes, hoping that as the cold evening came on the guards might let us come back. They knew we had children with us and, even though spring, it still often got below zero at night. They wouldn't let us freeze to death we thought. Surely they would let us go back. . . .

It was now late afternoon, probably around four or five o'clock. We huddled in conference as to what to do, for already there was a chill in the air. . . .

. . . Cautiously we climbed to the top of the arroyo so I could point out the Lowe house. I went on to explain: "The railroad company has an abandoned dry well near there. Mrs. Lowe takes care of it. I think it's about half a mile from here. She showed it to me once. . . ."

We convinced the children who could walk how important it was not to cry "so those bad men won't know where we are going." . . . We started up the muddy arroyo, slipping and sliding as we went along.

The guards hadn't been shooting toward the spot in the arroyo where we'd been all day. But as we went further up, crouching in some places not to be seen, the shots sounded very near. . . .

It was dusk when we neared the well. Out of nowhere a man's voice came, "Who goes there?" I turned white, thinking it might be a guard. "There are only women and children here," I faltered. Then a man with a rifle came forward. He was one of the miners who was guarding the tent colony. Others were about three hundred feet off on the other side of a knoll. I told him we were going to put the children in the well to keep warm.

He said, "You can't put them in there until a freight train comes along to hide you from the guards. They are right straight across from us, shooting at anything they see moving." He pulled a railroad schedule from his pocket. "There'll be a train going through in about an hour. I'll give it the signal to go slow so we can get you out of here fast."

"I'm going ahead along the arroyo to that house over there," I told him, "to get food and milk. . . ."

I crouched along and finally reached the Lowe house. I was covered with mud. Mrs. Lowe embraced me with tears in her eyes. . . .

". . . I came to ask you for food and milk for the children, if you have it to spare." . . .

. . . [Mrs. Lowe gave me] a big bag of cheese, loaves of bread, a chunk of butter, a gallon of milk and a gallon of water, a gallon of coffee, and she even thought of including eating utensils and a lantern. She had also made a sack of sandwiches for the miners, to wash down with a half gallon of coffee. Mr. Lowe added some tobacco and matches. All of this was as much as he and I could carry. . . .

The mile long freight train was wending its way toward us. Mr. Lowe crawled over the side of the arroyo to remove the padlock from the trap door of the well. Then he ran back home so the trainmen wouldn't see him helping the strikers. It could have meant his job. Many of the stock holders who controlled the mines controlled the railroad too, and railroad jobs were hard to get at that time.

As the train approached, the miner gave a signal to the engineer, and the engineer returned it. The "coded" signal was understood. They all had to be cautious to protect their jobs. The train slowed. As it passed at a snail's pace we made a dash for the well as it obscured us from the guards' vision.

Margo and I told the other women to go down first, and gave them the lantern to light. Then we began to hand down the children. Next we passed along the food to feed our hungry tots. . . . [I said,] "Look after my girls while I dash over to the knoll with the sandwiches and coffee for the miners." I barely made it before the last car of the train pulled by, accelerating as it went.

The men were very appreciative because they were cold and hungry too. . . . Yet even while enjoying his smoke, each miner kept an eye on the colony, rifle ready at his side.

After serving them, I took a sandwich and some coffee and sat on a rock to relax as much as I could while I ate. There were three of our miners staked out here whom I recognized by face although I didn't know their names. . . . One, the leader, was a big fellow who did little talking and seemed a serious man. The other two were much younger. . . .

These three miners had a good view of our tents from the knoll. The guards had tried to come into our camp, they told me, two and three at a time. But the miners were determined to keep them out and sniped at them when they came too close. . . .

. . . "You're not going to kill any of the guards, are you?" I asked.

"No, we just want to aim over their heads or at their heels to let them know we're watching out for our tents so they won't try to loot them."

We were beginning to run out of ammunition, and it was getting so dark I could hardly see who the miners were shooting at. We heard only the crackling of the guards' rifles, and the nearer sound of shots from our men in the nearby hills. . . .

. . . The younger men took up their rifles when the big miner looked through his spy-glass and told them . . . guards [were] taking things out of the tents. . . .

The big miner screamed, "Oh God! Now the tents are on fire!" We scrambled to the top of the knoll and moaned as we looked down on our flaming homes. . . .

One tent after another was set on fire. The colony became a blazing inferno. . . .

The leader broke the deathly pall. "Mrs. Thomas, those women and children in the well must be moved. . . . I don't suppose by now Louie can get ammunition to us. . . . It won't be long before they'll be up to get us. They know we're here from our shots."

. . . He pointed toward some hills in the distance. "About two miles in that direction there's a ranch. The people who live on it are friendly to the miners. There will be food and water for you until you can get help." . . .

. . . I crawled back to the well to tell the women that the strike was probably lost. That was bad enough, but how could I tell them that their homes were gone too. I was in a daze. Everything we had was in those tents. Most of us had brought beautiful, highly valued things from our own countries. Now all that any of us had was the tattered cotton dress on our back. I lifted the trap door quietly, went down into the well. . . .

Now all of the wild-eyed women were looking up at me from below. Margo started up the ladder, and as she reached the top of the well she saw the tent colony ablaze. . . .

The rest of the women scrambled up the ladders. Their moans were pitiful, like whimpering animals, when they saw the inferno of their homes. . . . Some were saying "what will become of us now?" and others were crying silently in despair.

. . . The women wondered anxiously about their husbands. When I told Margo that [our friend] Charley [Costa] had been killed she made the sign of the cross and began to sob silently, tears pouring down her cheeks.

It must have been around eleven o'clock when we heard the train whistle in the distance. We woke the older children after deciding to carry the sleeping babies so they wouldn't cry. . . . The miners arrived at the well just as the freight came to a screeching halt.

. . . Everything went like clockwork. The babies were handed to the miners who rushed them to the women already in the arroyo, and the rest of us helped herd the older ones quickly to safety there in the shadow of the train. The miners ran back to their knoll before it pulled away down the tracks.

Next morning the bullet riddled bodies of these three heroic men who helped us escape were found there.

We began our trek through the arroyo to the open prairie out of the danger zone, carrying the sleeping babies in our arms. . . . Once out on the prairie we wandered for miles through brush. . . .

We had lost our way. The children began to cry from thirst and exhaustion and fright. We were getting desperate, and the cold chilled us to the bone.

Suddenly one of the women said, "Isn't that a light over there?"

. . . We hurried our pace toward the haven of the light, even though we were so tired that we didn't think we could take another step. We had to pull the children along so they wouldn't fall asleep.

At last we reached the ranch and we were welcomed with open arms. It was packed with refugees from Ludlow. . . .

. . . Mr. and Mrs. Bates, who owned the ranch, made room for us and brought hot milk for the children and coffee for us. They had fed so many there wasn't a scrap of food left but a neighbor from another ranch near by would be bringing some soon. . . .

. . . We thanked kind Mrs. Bates for taking us in. She smiled and put her arm around me. "After all you have been through, it's the very least we can do to help as best we can. Get a good sleep, ladies." . . . Sleep, wonderful sleep, would make me feel like a human being again. But exhausted as I was I couldn't sleep. I was too tense and my body throbbed. I had to keep a firm hold on myself to keep from screaming hysterically. . . .

I racked my brain as to what work I could do to support my children, knowing no trade, everything gone. I had held my nerve until now without a tear, but felt on the verge of hysteria. . . .

I went down on my knees, looking up at the windowless opening to the skies. Never had I prayed so sincerely for God's help. My tears now flowed freely. I don't know how long I was there on my knees lost in meditation and prayer, but I saw the sun rising on another day. I got up and turned around. There was Margo on her knees along with the other women.

We were all of different nationalities and faiths . . . but our prayers were universal, and spoken to the same God.

26

PEARL JOLLY

Under Fire in the Ludlow Tent Colony
1914

Pearl Jolly was working as a hospital nurse in Colorado when she met her husband, a Scottish miner who went on strike in the fall of 1913. At age twenty-one, Jolly became the camp nurse and one of the key community leaders in Ludlow. During the April 20 siege, strike leaders asked her to stay in the tent camp and minister to the wounded, and she later helped dozens of women and children escape to a nearby ranch. A month later, she and two other women traveled to Washington, D.C., to tell their stories to the Commission on Industrial Relations.

From my first experience in the Ludlow tent colony the gunmen [soldiers and mine guards] would come there and would try in every way to provoke trouble. They were trying to cause a battle between the miners and the gunmen, but we knew that and we did not want to have any trouble. At one time the gunmen came to the Ludlow tent colony, just as near as they could get, fired two shots into the tent colony. Our men took their rifles and went to the hills, thinking that by so doing they would lead the fire that way and keep them from firing on the colony, where the women and children were. There was no way to protect the women and children. After that our men took and dug pits under the tents, so that if the same thing should happen again there would be some means of escape for those women and children. . . .

From U.S. Commission on Industrial Relations, *Final Report and Testimony* (Washington, D.C., 1916), 7: 6348–51.

On April 19[, 1914] we had a baseball game. The militia had always been in the habit of attending the baseball games, but never before had they attended with their rifles. On April 19 was a Greek holiday, Sunday, and they thought perhaps that they would be drinking, and those men, if they were to go down there with their rifles, would be able to stir up some trouble. They stood right in the diamond with their rifles. One of the men asked them if they would please get out of the diamond. He told them if he wanted to watch the baseball game it was not necessary to guard them, to put their guns to their side. They became indignant and made their threats what they could do and what they would not do. One of the women said to them, in a joke, "Don't you know if a woman would start toward you with a BB gun you would all throw away your guns and run." He says, "That is all right, girlie, you have your big Sunday to-day, but we will have the roast to-morrow. . . ."

They put guards in our camps Sunday night to take care of the camp, but nothing happened. On the following Monday morning, about 9 o'clock, the same five militiamen who had been at the baseball game on Sunday came to the Ludlow grounds. They had a paper and they sent in for Louis Tikas, a Greek and the leader; they handed him this slip of paper, and it had some foreign name on it of some man that was not in the tent colony. They told him they wanted to take the man out of the colony; [he asked them] if they had a warrant or had been sent there by the civil authorities. They said no, they had been sent there by the military authorities. They said, "I understand the military commission is out now." He says, "I would like to talk to Manager Hemrock [Major Hamrock]," who was in command. So they left the Ludlow tent colony with a threat that they would be back again. When they met Louis Tikas they went and called up Manager Hemrock and asked him if he would see him and talk to him. He said he would. They met at the C. & S. depot. I don't know what the conversation was at the depot, but I know when Louis Tikas came back he told us the machine guns and everything were set ready to wipe the tent colony. The next thing we observed was Louis Tikas coming from the depot waiving a white handkerchief. There was about 200 tents in the tent colony and about 1,000 inhabitants, about 500 women and 500 children. We were all in front in large groups. He was waiving this white handkerchief, I suppose, for us to get back. While he was running toward us and waiving the white handkerchief they fired two bombs. Following that they turned the machine gun into the tent colony and started to firing with rifles. Our men decided if they would take the hills, take their rifles and go into the hills, that they would lead fire from the tent colony into the hills and thus protect the women and children in the tent colony. There was just 40 rifles in the Ludlow camp. They will tell you there was 500 or so. There was 40 in there, and I would swear to that before any jury in the United States. The men who had rifles went to the hills, and the others, too, so that there would not be any men in the camp, thinking in that way they would attract the fire away from the women and children. Then if no men were there they would not fire. They did not follow the men into the hills; they were too cowardly; they wanted to fight with the women. They kept the machine guns turned on the camp all day, more or less. The women and children, too, could run out of the camp, but there were so many women there expecting to become mothers, and also many that had such a large family of small children that they could not possibly get out. I had been the nurse in the tent colony. Louis Tikas came to me and told me if I was not afraid he wanted me to stay in the camp and take care of the wounded and the women and children.

When they kept continually shooting into the camp the women asked me to put a white dress on with red crosses. I was afraid to do it, but I did it and went out to the front and pinned a red cross on each arm and one on my chest; they could not help but see it. When I got out there they took it for to be a good target and shot at me as hard as they could. I started to run for protection, and one of the bullets took the heel off my shoe. I thought at first it had shot my foot off. A little while later I went into my tent. . . .

Another time that day there was a wounded man in the camp, and I was trying to get to the dispensary to get some dressing for him. I couldn't get there at first, because the bullets were coming in there like hail. The second time they decided that if Louis Tikas would go with me and unlock the door quick I could get in there quick. He went out, and they saw us when we got about half way and opened fire. There was a small coal pile there, but that was no protection for even one man, but we both dodged behind it. We lay still for two or three minutes and thought they would stop, and they did stop, but they started again; but they were setting the machine gun on us, and we didn't have sense enough to know it. In about three minutes there were three men lying there with us back of the coal pile. We were laying there flat on the ground behind this little coal pile. They kept the machine gun on us I don't know how long, but it seemed like an awful long time, but I think it was about an hour steady. The bullets were hitting just about a foot on the other side of us. They did not have the range right. I don't understand how we ever got out of there alive at the time the machine gun was trained on us. There was a little 12-year-old boy shot in the tent colony. The father came out to tell us. When he came out he took the machine gun off of us long enough to chase him back to the tent, and that is how we made our escape, through that. From about 3 o'clock on it was worse than ever.

They got the machine gun set better and at better range, for it was terrible how those bullets came in there; it does not seem possible to tell how they were coming in. They would say if the bullets were coming in like that, why were there not more shot? Simply because the caves [the pits under the tents] were there and the dogs and chickens and everything else that moved were shot. Between 5 and 6 o'clock they set fire to our tents. When they set fire to our tents we decided that we would go from cave to cave as fast as we could. They could see us going through, and we had to dodge their bullets. We were going from cave to cave, getting the women and children together, and let them out, and took chances on being shot. . . . I believe you could hear [the screams] for a mile. The screams of the women and children—they were simply awful. . . .

There were three of our men captured and murdered while they were trying to rescue those women and children. Two out of the three did not have revolvers. One of the men had a rifle. He had been out and came back and got his wife and family out. At the time this fire broke out our men quit camping altogether. They thought I had made a run for the tent—meant to get the children out—and I made my way leading to this farmhouse. When this little boy was shot, his mother said they had not had a bite to eat that day. None of us had any breakfast that morning. Yet, not one-half of the people in the tent colony were up and dressed. If we were planning a battle like they say we were, it is most certain that the women would have been dressed and ready to get out.

27

WILLIAM SNYDER

Affidavit Given to the Commission on Industrial Relations

1914

William Snyder was one of the operators of the Ludlow general store that served the strikers' camp. A resident of the Ludlow tent colony himself, he left the store on the morning of April 20 and returned to camp to protect his wife and family. His eleven-year-old son, Frank, was one of the people killed in the attack. Snyder described this traumatic event in an affidavit taken by investigators from the Commission on Industrial Relations.

I myself, not being armed, stayed on the tent colony grounds to protect my family to the best of my ability, and that about 4:30 P.M. when the thugs or the militia had right-flanked our colony and shot through my tent and killed our boy, showing clearly that they did not stop to see whether there were any women or children on the colony ground or not; just previous to the time the boy was shot he got out of the hole or cave, where my children were, to get his sister a drink of water, and as the firing had slackened the children had left the hole, being out of the hole from five to eight minutes, and stepped into the bedroom of my tent, the boy Frank was sitting in the chair with his sister on the floor between his knees, and he was in the act of stooping to kiss or caress his sister, when the bullet struck him above the temple on the right side and blew his brains out. I was standing near the front door of my tent and I heard the impact of the bullet striking the boy's head, and the crack of the bullet as it exploded inside of his head. The boy was killed by an explosive bullet. I went to the boy to render what assistance I could, and while falling I caught him in my arms and in the act of letting him down to the floor, two more bullets passed over me in the tent; then I went to the hole where my family

From U.S. Commission on Industrial Relations, *Final Report and Testimony* (Washington, D.C., 1916), 8: 7377–79.

and children were, and seeing the boy in his death struggles went to him again, was in the act of washing his face, when another bullet went over me, the firing became so heavy that I went to my family and stayed in the cave with them until they burned the tents. They fired this tent of mine by standing by the S.W. corner with a piece of paper on fire in their hands, and as the tent was blazing they came in the tent. This I observed by looking out of the hole where we were located. As the tent was in flames, they opened the door and came in and then my wife pleaded to save her children, telling them they had already killed one, and for God sake to save the others. Whereupon this officer assisted Mrs. Snyder from the hole, and the other children. By this time there was five or six militia or thugs in the tent, and wanted to kill me. And I asked of them to let me get my dead boy to the Depot, and to which this officer consented, after cursing me, putting a gun to my head and threatening to kill me, and on leaving the tent with the corpse I laid him down outside of the door to put on my coat and I requested of someone to help me carry this boy to the depot. When I was told that I was big enough to carry him myself, and which I did over my shoulder and my $3\frac{1}{2}$ year old daughter in my arms, when George Titsworth Sr. who to the best of my knowledge set fire to my tent, throwed a gun on me and said "You god dam dirty sun of a bitch, I ought to kill you right here, you have fired as many shots as anybody" and he touched my head, or nearly so with his revolver and said "I will kill you." My wife pleaded in behalf of her dead boy to let us get him to Trinidad, and this officer supported us to the depot. But on passing Snodgrass store at Ludlow, [Lieutenant] Linderfelt threw his flash light in my face, and wanted to know what "god damn red neck S.B." they had here, when Mrs. Snyder says to Linderfelt "Please don't shoot him, they have killed one of my children already" when Linderfelt says "It is a damn pity that all of you damn red necked bitches were not killed."

28

GODFREY IRWIN

The Killing of Louis Tikas

1914

Godfrey Irwin, an electrical engineer employed by a local railroad, was passing through the hills above Ludlow when the fighting broke out on April 20. He was the only nonmilitary witness to the killing of the Greek union leader, Louis Tikas, and he also described the firing of the Ludlow tent camp. He was subsequently interviewed by a reporter for the New York World, *which published his account two weeks later. The interview was also included in a 1914 UMWA report titled "The Ludlow Massacre," the name by which the events of April 20 came to be known thereafter.*

"We were going down a trail on the mountain side above the tent city at Ludlow when my chum pulled my sleeve and at the same instant we heard shooting. The militia were coming out of Hastings Canyon and firing as they came. We lay flat behind a rock and after a few minutes I raised my hat aloft on a stick. Instantly bullets came in our direction. One penetrated my hat. The militiamen must have been watching the hillside through glasses and thought my old hat betrayed the whereabouts of a sharpshooter of the miners.

"Then came the killing of Louis Tikas, the Greek leader of the strikers. We saw the militiamen parley outside the tent city, and, a few minutes later, Tikas came out to meet them. We watched them talking. Suddenly an officer raised his rifle, gripping the barrel, and felled Tikas with the butt.

"Tikas fell face downward. As he lay there we saw the militiamen fall back. Then they aimed their rifles and deliberately fired them into the unconscious man's body. It was the first murder I had ever seen, for it was a murder and nothing less. Then the miners ran about in the tent colony and women and children scuttled for safety in the pits which afterward trapped them.

From Walter H. Fink, District 15 UMWA, "The Ludlow Massacre," in *Massacre at Ludlow: Four Reports*, ed. Leon Stein and Philip Taft (New York: Arno Press, 1971), 22–23.

"We watched from our rock shelter while the militia dragged up their machine guns and poured a murderous fire into the arroyo from a height by Water Tank Hill above the Ludlow depot. Then came the firing of the tents.

"I am positive that by no possible chance could they have been set ablaze accidentally. The militiamen were thick about the northwest corner of the colony where the fire started and we could see distinctly from our lofty observation place what looked like a blazing torch waved in the midst of militia a few seconds before the general conflagration swept through the place. What followed everybody knows.

"Sickened by what we had seen, we took a freight back into Trinidad. The town buzzed with indignation. To explain in large part the sympathies of even the best people in the section with the miners, it must be said that there is good evidence that many of the so-called 'militiamen' are only gunmen and thugs wearing the uniform to give them a show of authority. They are the toughest lot I ever saw."

29

JOHN SLOAN

Class War in Colorado

1914

This striking image by the artist John Sloan appeared on the cover of the June 1914 issue of The Masses, *a radical literary magazine based in New York. The cover image accompanied an article by editor Max Eastman about Ludlow and the callous attitudes of the coal operators and their families in the wake of the tragedy. Sloan's drawing, by contrast, sought to explain the bitter and violent reactions of the strikers, who continued to battle the militia and company guards for weeks after the conflagration at the tent camp.*

The Masses, June 1914, front cover.

JUNE, 1914   10 CENTS

MASSES

IN THIS ISSUE
CLASS WAR IN COLORADO—Max Eastman
WHAT ABOUT MEXICO?—John Reed

30

JOHN D. ROCKEFELLER JR.

Labor and Capital—Partners

1916

Although the strike ended in defeat for the United Mine Workers, the magnitude of the Ludlow tragedy attracted national attention and stirred extensive public debate over labor and industrial conditions. The negative publicity surrounding Ludlow and the damaging report by the U.S. Commission on Industrial Relations convinced John D. Rockefeller Jr. to launch a campaign to repair Colorado Fuel and Iron's image. The centerpiece of this effort was the Colorado Industrial Representation Plan, devised with the help of Mackenzie King, a Canadian labor mediator who would later become prime minister. The plan, described by Rockefeller in this Atlantic Monthly *article, called for a form of company-sponsored industrial governance that included both workers and management. Implemented at CFI later that year, the plan proved influential among corporate managers, who went on to create company-sponsored unions, vacation and benefit plans, and corporate welfare activities such as sports teams, newspapers, and lunchrooms. This movement, known as welfare capitalism, would become especially popular in the 1920s as part of employers' efforts to undercut unions. Historians continue to debate the plan's ultimate aims and impact.*

Our difficulty in dealing with the industrial problem is due too often to a failure to understand the true interests of Labor and Capital. And I suspect this lack of understanding is just as prevalent among representatives of Capital as among representatives of Labor. In any event the conception one has of the fundamental nature of these interests will naturally determine one's attitude toward every phase of their relationship.

Much of the reasoning on this subject proceeds upon the theory that the wealth of the world is absolutely limited, and that if one man

From John D. Rockefeller Jr., "Labor and Capital—Partners," *Atlantic Monthly*, January 1916, 12–19.

gets more, another necessarily gets less. Hence there are those who hold that if Labor's wages are increased or its working conditions improved, Capital suffers because it must deprive itself of the money needed to pay the bill. Some employers go so far as to justify themselves in appropriating from the product of industry all that remains after Labor has received the smallest amount which it can be induced or forced to accept; while on the other hand there are men who hold that Labor is the producer of all wealth, hence is entitled to the entire product, and that whatever is taken by Capital is stolen from Labor.

If this theory is sound, it might be maintained that the relation between Labor and Capital is fundamentally one of antagonism, and that each should consolidate and arm its forces, dividing the products of industry between them in proportion as their selfishness is enforced by their power.

But all such counsel loses sight of the fact that the riches available to man are practically without limit; that the world's wealth is constantly being developed and undergoing mutation, and that to promote this process both Labor and Capital are indispensable. If these great forces coöperate, the products of industry are steadily increased; whereas, if they fight, the production of wealth is certain to be either retarded or stopped altogether, and the wellsprings of material progress choked. The problem of promoting the coöperation of Labor and Capital may well be regarded, therefore, as the most vital problem of modern civilization. . . .

With reference to the situation which had unfortunately developed in Colorado, it became evident to those responsible for the management of one of the larger coal companies there—the Colorado Fuel & Iron Company, in which my father and I are interested—that matters could not be allowed to remain as they were. Any situation, no matter what its cause, out of which so much bitterness could grow, clearly required amelioration.

It has always been the desire and purpose of the management of the Colorado Fuel & Iron Company that its employees should be treated liberally and fairly. However, it became clear that there was need of some more efficient method whereby the petty frictions of daily work might be dealt with promptly and justly, and of some machinery which, without imposing financial burdens upon the workers, would protect the rights, and encourage the expression of the wants and aspirations of the men—not merely of those men who were members of some organization, but of every man on the company's payroll. The problem was . . . how to foster at the same time the interest of both the stockholders and the employees through bringing them to realize the fact of their real partnership.

Long before the Colorado strike ended, I sought advice with respect to possible methods of preventing and adjusting such a situation as that which had arisen; and in December, 1914, as soon as the strike was terminated and normal conditions were restored, the officers of the Colorado Fuel & Iron Company undertook the practical development of plans which had been under consideration. The men in each mining camp were invited to choose, by secret ballot, representatives to meet with the executive officers of the company to discuss matters of mutual concern and consider means of more effective coöperation in maintaining fair and friendly relations.

That was the beginning, merely the germ, of a plan which has now been developed into a comprehensive "Industrial Constitution." The scheme embodies practical operating experience, the advice and study of experts, and an earnest effort to provide a workable method of friendly consideration, by all concerned, of the daily problems which arise in the mutual relations between employer and employees.

The plan was submitted to a referendum of the employees in all the company's coal and iron mines, and adopted by an overwhelming vote. Before this general vote was taken, it had been considered and unanimously approved by a meeting of the employees' elected representatives. At that meeting I outlined the plan, which is described below. . . .

Every corporation is composed of four parties: the stockholders, who supply the money with which to build the plant, pay the wages, and operate the business; the directors, whose duty it is to select executive officers carefully and wisely, plan the larger and more important policies, and generally see to it that the company is prudently administered; the officers, who conduct the current operations, and the employees, who contribute their skill and their work. The interest of these four parties is a common interest, although perhaps not an equal one. . . . An effort on the part of any one to advance its own interest without regard to the rights of the others, means, eventually, loss to all. The problem which confronts every company is so to interrelate its different elements that the best interests of all will be conserved.

The industrial machinery which has been adopted by the Colorado Fuel & Iron Company and its employees is embodied in two written documents, which have been printed and placed in the hands of each employee. One of these documents is a trade agreement signed by the representatives of the men and the officers of the company, setting forth the conditions and terms under which the men agree to work until January 1, 1918, and thereafter, subject to revision upon ninety days' notice by either side. This agreement guarantees to the men that for more than two years, no matter what reductions in wages others may make, there shall be no reduction of wages by this company; furthermore, that in the event of an increase in wages in any competitive field, this company will make a proportional increase.

The agreement provides for an eight-hour day for all employees working underground and in coke ovens; it insures the semi-monthly payment of wages; it fixes charges for such dwellings, light, and water, as are provided by the company; it stipulates that the rates to be charged for powder and coal used by the men shall be substantially their cost to the company. To encourage employees to cultivate flower and vegetable gardens, the company agrees to fence free of cost each house-lot owned by it. The company also engages to provide suitable bathhouses and clubhouses for the use of employees at the several mining camps.

The other document is an "Industrial Constitution," setting forth the relations of the company and its men. The constitution stipulates, among other things, that "there shall be a strict observance by management and men of the federal and state laws respecting mining and labor," and that "the scale of wages and the rules in regard to working conditions shall be posted in a conspicuous place at or near every mine." Every employee is protected against discharge without notice, except for such offenses as are posted at each mine. . . .

The constitution specifically states that "there shall be no discrimination by the company or any of its employees on account of membership or nonmembership in any society, fraternity, or union." The employees are guaranteed the right to hold meetings on company property, to purchase where they choose, and to employ check-weighmen, who, on behalf of the men, shall see to it that each gets proper credit for his work.

Besides setting forth these fundamental rights of the men, the industrial constitution seeks to establish a recognized means for bringing the management and the men into closer contact for two general purposes: first, to promote increased efficiency and production, to improve working conditions, and to further the friendly and cordial relations between the company's officers and employees; and, second, to facilitate the adjustment of disputes and the redress of grievances.

In carrying out this plan, the wage-earners at each camp are to be represented by two or more of their own number chosen by secret

ballot, at meetings especially called for the purpose, which none but
wage-earners in the employ of the company shall be allowed to attend.
The men thus chosen are to be recognized by the company as authorized to represent the employees for one year, or until their successors
are elected, with respect to terms of employment, working and living
conditions, adjustment of differences, and such other matters as may
come up. A meeting of all the men's representatives and the general
officers of the company will be held once a year to consider questions
of general importance.

The Industrial Constitution provides that the territory in which the
company operates shall be divided into a number of districts based on
the geographical distribution of the mines. . . .

The district conferences will each appoint from their number certain joint committees on industrial relations, and it is expected that
these committees will give prompt and continuous attention to the
many questions which affect the daily life and happiness of the men as
well as the prosperity of the company. . . . A joint committee on industrial coöperation and conciliation will consider matters pertaining
to the prevention and settlement of industrial disputes, terms and
conditions of employment, maintenance of order and discipline in the
several camps, policy of the company stores, and so forth. Joint committees on safety and accidents, on sanitation, health and housing, on
recreation and education, will likewise deal with the great variety of
topics included within these general designations.

Prevention of friction is an underlying purpose of the plan. The aim
is to anticipate and remove in advance all sources of possible irrita-
tion. With this in view a special officer, known as the President's
Industrial Representative, is added to the personnel of the staff as a
further link between the President of the corporation and every workman in his employ. This officer's duty is to respond promptly to
requests from employees' representatives for his presence at any of
the camps, to visit all of them as often as possible, to familiarize himself with conditions, and generally to look after the well-being of the
workers.

It is a fundamental feature of the plan, as stated in the document
itself, that "every employee shall have the right of ultimate appeal to
the president of the company concerning any condition or treatment
to which he may be subjected and which he may deem unfair." . . . If
any miner has a grievance, he may himself, or preferably through one
of the elected representatives in his camp, seek satisfaction from the
foreman or mine superintendent. If those officials do not adjust the

matter, appeal may be had to the president's industrial representative. Failing there, the employee may appeal to the division superintendent, assistant manager, manager, or general manager, or the president of the company, in consecutive order. Yet another alternative is that, after having made the initial complaint to the foreman or mine superintendent, the workman may appeal directly to the joint committee on industrial coöperation and conciliation in his district, which, itself failing to agree, may select one or three umpires, whose decision shall be binding upon both parties to the dispute. If all these methods of mediation fail the employee may appeal to the Colorado State Industrial Commission, which is empowered by law to investigate industrial disputes and publish its findings.

So as adequately to protect the independence and freedom of the men's representatives, the Constitution provides that in case any one of them should be discharged or disciplined, or should allege discrimination, he may resort to the various methods of appeal open to the other employees, or he may appeal directly to the Colorado State Industrial Commission, with whose findings in any such case the company agrees to comply.

The company is to pay all expenses incident to the administration of the plan, and to reimburse the miners' representatives for loss of time from their work in the mines.

Such in outline is this Industrial Constitution. Some have spoken of it as establishing a Republic of Labor. Certain it is that the plan gives every employee opportunity to voice his complaints and aspirations, and it neglects no occasion to bring the men and the managers together to talk over their common interests.

Much unrest among employees is due to the nursing of real or fancied grievances arising out of the daily relations between the workmen and the petty boss. Such grievances should receive attention at once, and this plan provides that they shall.

PART THREE

Epilogue: Remembering Johnson County and Ludlow

Numerous Americans, from presidents to hip-hop artists, have drawn on the symbolism and rhetoric of the Wild West and the public's fascination with western violence to promote everything from music to warfare. The popular appeal of frontier violence dates back to the mid-nineteenth century. Stories of western cowboys, outlaws, and lawmen first appeared in the dime novels of the 1860s and were later dramatized in the Wild West shows of Buffalo Bill Cody and others. Before long, Hollywood recognized the profitability of western violence and produced films based on fictionalized accounts of frontier history. In popular literature, film, music, and television, the western genre has proved remarkably resilient, incorporating and interpreting new social and political trends across more than a century.

Curiously, some types of western violence have been more popular than others. In particular, the range wars have been the subject of sustained fascination, with hundreds of books, movies, and TV shows recounting the saga of cattlemen, rustlers, homesteaders, and vigilantes and their violent showdowns. Although these stories have changed over the years to reflect new social mores, the appeal of the range war as a metaphor for American society has been irresistible. By contrast, the mining wars have attracted little attention. Despite the critical plight of western mining families and compelling sagas such as the Ludlow strike and massacre, there are few books or films about the mining wars that wracked the West for more than thirty years. Both the mining and range wars were dramatic examples of class and ethnic conflict in the West, yet our historical recollection of the range wars is far stronger. A brief examination of popular depictions of the two events may shed some light on this disparity.

Even before the Johnson County War ended, accounts of its violent confrontations had become grist for Wyoming storytellers. In the early 1890s, Wyoming settlers penned folk ballads vilifying the vigilantes and celebrating their victims in songs such as "The Ballad of Cattle Kate," "The Murder of Tisdale and Jones," and "Our Heroes' Graves." The most popular tune was "The Invasion Song," a tribute to Nate Champion and others who fought the regulators (Document 16). Disparaging the cattlemen "and their murderous crew," the song pays homage to "poor Nate and Nick, who gave their precious lives, / To save the town of Buffalo, its brave men and their wives." Wyoming newspaper editors such as Asa Shinn Mercer and Jack Flagg wrote book-length accounts of the Johnson County War (Documents 4, 8, 10, and 15) that were equally sympathetic to settlers. At the height of the western populist movement in the 1890s, such paeans to little guys struggling against wealthy eastern interests were distinctly appealing.

Populist enthusiasm for the victims of the Johnson County War was not widely shared elsewhere. In 1902, author Owen Wister presented a different view of the conflict in his best-selling novel *The Virginian* (Figure 5). Published a decade after the Johnson County War, the book was loosely based on the events of 1892 and included characters modeled on Wyoming cattlemen that Wister encountered in his travels. His Virginia-born hero is a Wyoming cowhand who confronts cattle rustlers led by the black-hatted Trampas. The Virginian joins a lynching party in hanging some of the gang. Trampas escapes but later

---

(opposite) **Figure 5.** *Range Wars in Popular Culture*
Loosely based on the Johnson County War, Owen Wister's 1902 novel *The Virginian* pits a Virginia-born hero against a dangerous band of cattle rustlers led by a villain named Trampas. *The Virginian* became a western literary classic that spawned numerous theatrical adaptations, including a Broadway play, several films, and a 1960s television program. In 1959 Classics Illustrated published a comic book based on Wister's novel. Its cover featured the dramatic walk down and shoot-out on Main Street—a scene that had become a cinematic cliché in Hollywood westerns.

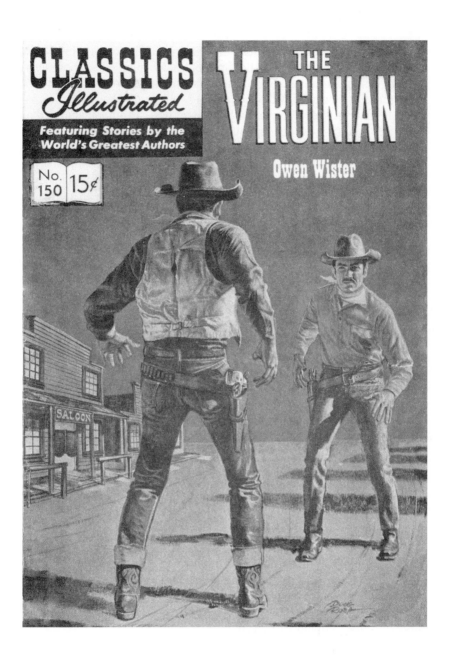

turns up in town and encounters the Virginian. The two proceed to a shoot-out on Main Street—the first of many such classic western scenes. Killing Trampas, the Virginian has made the West safe for civilization and is rewarded with the love of Molly Stark Wood, an eastern lady. He marries her, abandoning his violent past. The book soon led to theatrical adaptations, one opening on Broadway in 1904, as well as numerous film versions, including silent productions in 1914 and 1923 and a sound version starring Gary Cooper in 1929. A later film incarnation of *The Virginian* appeared in 1946, and a made-for-TV movie came out in 2000. Each time, the Johnson County conflict was refashioned so that the Virginian represents the forces of order and civilization against a wild and criminal element of Wyoming rustlers. Well suited to the pro-business climate of the 1920s (when the most influential film version appeared), *The Virginian* reflects the incorporators' view of western history, in which the forces of capitalism make the West safe for civilization.[1]

After World War II, however, most popular depictions of the Johnson County War favored the anti-incorporator viewpoint. This shift began with the 1949 publication of *Shane*, a western novel by Jack Schaefer. Released as a Hollywood film starring Alan Ladd in 1953, *Shane* was among the most successful movies of the 1950s and became one of the most famous westerns of all time. In it, hardworking homesteaders on the Wyoming range square off against arrogant and greedy cattlemen known as the Ryker brothers. As the Rykers try to bully the settlers off their claims, the homesteaders find an ally in Shane, a gun-toting drifter who works for the Starrett family. A virile character with a shadowy past, Shane tries to settle down and forswear his violent ways. But the intensifying violence on the range moves him to defend the Starretts and other homesteaders who want to tame the frontier for independent farmers. Eventually, Shane shoots it out with Jack Wilson, a hired gunman from Cheyenne, killing both Wilson and the Rykers before riding off wounded into the mountains. The triumph of the noble homesteaders was a comforting outcome for a postwar audience of suburban homeowners, but the film's struggle between civilized domesticity and manly toughness reflected the gender insecurities of the cold war, when the need to "stand up to the Russians" preoccupied Americans.

[1] Richard Maxwell Brown, "Violence," in *The Oxford History of the American West*, ed. Clyde Milner, Carol O'Connor, and Martha A. Sandweiss (New York: Oxford University Press, 1994), 419–21. *The Virginian* was also the title of a popular TV western in the 1960s, but little of Wister's original plot or characters survived.

Michael Cimino's infamous 1980 film *Heaven's Gate* also reflects the neo-populist view of the Johnson County War, but with a twist. Cimino transformed the homesteaders into impoverished eastern European immigrants who unwittingly settle on Wyoming rangelands controlled by British and American cattle barons. Viewing the immigrant home-steaders as "thieves, rustlers, and anarchists," the cattle association launches an invasion, aided by the U.S. cavalry. In Cimino's version, the U.S. government is complicit in the capitalist takeover of the West, and the plight of the homesteaders is aggravated by their identity as racial outsiders. Although the film is purportedly based on the Johnson County War, the immigrant dimension is fictional, and the characters—who bear the names of real historical figures—have little resemblance to those figures. Instead, *Heaven's Gate* can be seen as a post-1960s allegory of western conquest that anticipated themes of the New Western History emerging in the 1980s—racial and ethnic tensions, class conflict, and the vital role of women. Condemning the capitalist exploitation of the West, the film highlights the racial and class conflicts that fueled the range wars and other battles over western lands and resources. Reflecting the new feminist sensibilities of the 1970s, the film also offered women more instrumental roles, with "Cattle Kate" and other frontier women brandishing rifles and fighting alongside men. But its convoluted plot and disastrous production (the initial release ran more than three and a half hours and cost a record $40 million) made it a colossal cinematic flop.[2]

A more recent incarnation of the Wyoming range war appeared in a 2002 made-for-TV movie, *Johnson County War*. Based on Frederick Manfred's 1957 novel *Riders of Judgment*, the film portrays a more diverse array of wealthy cattlemen, hardscrabble homesteaders, and crafty rustlers. *Johnson County War* concentrates on personal and moral struggles between the three Hammett brothers (two of whom are honest homesteaders and one a rustler) and their desperate efforts to survive the cattle barons' deadly vigilante campaign. Interestingly, the U.S. government plays no role, and contrary to the actual events, the brothers get the best of the final gunfight at the TA Ranch, killing half a dozen regulators. Although Cain Hammett, the lead character, is eventually killed, the regulators surrender to the local sheriff and townspeople, with every indication that justice will be done. The film is thus a populist fantasy in which heroic homesteaders give their

[2]For budget and background on *Heaven's Gate*, see the Internet Movie Database, www.imdb.com/title/tt0080855 (accessed April 3, 2008).

lives in pursuing freedom and justice. It is perhaps no coincidence that in the conservative climate of the early twenty-first century, government is irrelevant to the story and its triumphant outcome.

Given the popular interest in the Johnson County War, Wyomingites have commemorated the event and use it to promote tourism. Most of the preservation efforts began with the 1990 Wyoming Centennial Project, including the establishment of the Hoofprints of the Past Museum in Kaycee, Wyoming (site of the old KC Ranch), and the erection of a nearby historical marker describing the killing of Nate Champion and Nick Ray. Along with the Jim Gatchell Memorial Museum in Buffalo, the Kaycee museum features exhibits on the Johnson County War and the area's violent past. In 1992 (the one hundredth anniversary of the conflict), a local Buffalo bank commissioned two bronze statues commemorating the Johnson County War. One, titled *Living on the Edge*, portrays an independent rancher branding a maverick calf. The other, titled *Ridin' for the Brand*, features a foreman or stock detective challenging the intruder. A commemorative brochure issued by the bank at the unveiling describes the Johnson County War in populist terms as a "conflict between the wealthy and the common man."[3]

Building on this upsurge in historic preservation, the owners of the TA Ranch transformed it into a guest ranch and conference center after purchasing it in 1991. Up to thirty guests can sleep in the original ranch house and outbuildings where the siege took place. The facilities have been sumptuously renovated to include cable TV, wireless Internet, and other amenities while preserving the ranch's key historic features, including bullet holes from the siege. Tourists raised on movies such as *Shane* and *The Virginian* can now spend a week horseback riding, cattle roping, or fly-fishing in the same setting where, according to the TA Web site, "a group of cattle barons set out to eliminate any threat to their control of the Powder River country by hunting down smaller independent ranchers."[4] As in Deadwood, South Dakota, western violence has been memorialized to promote tourism.

The views of history embodied in these tourist sites and popular accounts have changed over the years. Early-twentieth-century versions such as Owen Wister's *The Virginian* reflect the pro-expansion and pro-incorporation views of Anglo elites, celebrating the manly

---

[3] Bill O'Neal, *The Johnson County War* (Austin, Tex.: Eakin Press, 2004); First National Bank of Buffalo, *Johnson County Cattle War Commemorative Bronzes* (brochure, provided by the artist, D. Michael Thomas).

[4] Information on the TA Guest Ranch is available at www.taranch.com (accessed April 3, 2008).

conquest of the West and the triumph of civilization. After World War II, as racial minorities, women, and newly ascendant ethnic groups struggled for acceptance in American society, depictions of the Johnson County War became more sympathetic to the "little people" who fought against entrenched power and wealth (a stand long taken by many Wyoming residents). In these versions, greedy cattle barons target hardworking, independent settlers to preserve their unfair monopoly. Reflecting the social diversity celebrated by the civil rights movement, such accounts also feature assertive women, feisty immigrants, and an occasional black or Native American.

Interestingly, none of these accounts mentions that many of the cattlemen's key opponents were former employees who had fought with bosses over wage cuts, meal charges, and mavericking. Much of the history of class conflict is obscured, and the settlers are transformed into noble western homesteaders who fall prey to evil invaders. The settlers are portrayed as simple farmers trying to protect their families and property rights in the time-honored tradition of Jeffersonian America. They thus represent a long-standing view of the West as a bastion of rugged, independent men who defended themselves and their communities from outside threats and unwarranted power. Like *The Virginian*, these later accounts use the West as a metaphor for America as a land of independence and self-reliance. The earlier quest for mastery and civilization has been replaced by an updated view of American values stressing populist independence and manly fortitude in the face of a corrupt and bloated society. These accounts mesh well with the popular view of western history first put forth by the historian Frederick Jackson Turner back in 1893: the frontier as a region of "free land" and opportunity that inspired autonomy, resourcefulness, and democracy among its inhabitants.

Whereas the Johnson County War has aroused endless fascination, the Ludlow Massacre remains a distant memory. Although the events of the 1913–1914 strike are as compelling as those of the Johnson County range war and involved greater violence and death, there are only a couple of book-length accounts of the strike and massacre and no feature films, and few American history textbooks even mention it. Woody Guthrie wrote a ballad about Ludlow in the 1940s, but only a handful of left-wing singers ever performed it. This is not to say that Ludlow has been forgotten; local union members, labor activists, and sympathetic residents have worked diligently to keep its memory alive.

The most important guardians of this history are members of the United Mine Workers of America (UMWA). Two years after the

Colorado strike, UMWA officials purchased a forty-acre parcel of land where the Ludlow tent colony stood. Soon after, next to the infamous black hole [the pit beneath the tents where the bodies of the thirteen women and children were found], they built a memorial that included a plaque with the names and ages of the eighteen miners and their wives and children who died at Ludlow. The union also erected a granite sculpture of a miner with his wife and child under the inscription "In memory of the men, women and children, who lost their lives in freedom's cause at Ludlow, Colorado, April 20, 1914." The memorial was dedicated in the spring of 1918. Every year since then, a memorial ceremony has been held there in June, attracting a small but committed group of union supporters and local residents. Their goal is to honor the victims as labor heroes who gave their lives to win rights for working people that most Americans now take for granted. They also point to Ludlow as a symbol of oppression and resistance to bolster current labor struggles.[5]

Still, sustaining the public memory of Ludlow has been an uphill battle. The coal mining industry has long since left this part of the state, and a dwindling number of older residents recall work in the mines. Indeed, most visitors to the memorial stumble on it accidentally.

To recover the history of the strike, a group of archaeologists began excavating the Ludlow site in 1997. Uncovering tent platforms, pits where women and children took refuge, and an assortment of artifacts, the Colorado Coal Field War Project worked with the UMWA to interpret some of the lost history of the mining community. With funding from the State of Colorado, the project organized site tours, a traveling exhibit, and a teacher's institute designed to bring labor history into the K–12 curriculum.[6] Within the state, the project's work was an important step toward raising public awareness of coal mining communities and their history, but it has not led to any major rediscovery of Ludlow by the broader American public.

The failure to remember Ludlow is part of a larger public amnesia regarding U.S. labor history. Although social historians have written hundreds of volumes on the working class since the 1960s, surprisingly little of this history is being preserved in museums or at historic sites.

---

[5]Dean Saitta, Mark Walker, and Paul Reckner, "Battlefields of Class Conflict: Ludlow Then and Now," *Journal of Conflict Archaeology* 1 (2005): 204, 208; Mark Walker, "The Ludlow Massacre: Class, Warfare, and Historical Memory in Southern Colorado," *Historical Archaeology* 37 (Fall 2003): 72–73.

[6]Saitta, Walker, and Reckner, "Battlefields of Class Conflict," 209; Walker, "The Ludlow Massacre," 75.

The failure of the public to embrace labor history has been conditioned by a strong American myth of opportunity and social mobility that denies or minimizes class conflict.[7] Labor history is an especially hard sell in the West, where promises of free land and opportunity attracted generations of settlers and homesteaders. As Turner argued, the West was a safety valve for the simmering social discontent of the urban industrial East. In reality, however, the West was hardly immune from such troubles. As the history of Ludlow illustrates, western industrial development entailed the exploitation of a low-paid immigrant work-force and produced widespread industrial strife. Far from being a haven from eastern industrialization, the western economy was part of a global capitalist market and shared many of its problems.

This "wage-workers frontier," as one historian termed it, is not the West with which most Americans are familiar.[8] They would much prefer to think of western violence in terms of Indian battles, saloon fights, and range wars, narratives that confirm accepted notions of rugged in-dividualism, independence, and white frontier manhood. Moreover, the American promise of mobility, both social and geographic, is notably ab-sent from the miners' story. The dark, cramped confines of the mines and the social repression of the company town do not afford the same cinematic opportunities as the wide-open spaces and freewheeling cattle towns of the range wars. Images of tent camps full of dispos-sessed immigrant miners and their families waging a collective struggle against industrial exploitation hardly fits Hollywood's western bill.

The tendency to erase the memory of class conflict was strikingly evident in 2003 when the Ludlow memorial was vandalized. On May 8, the caretaker discovered that two of the granite figures had been decapitated (Figure 6). To assist the sheriffs department's investiga-tion of the crime, the UMWA offered a $5,000 reward. Many locals suspected that anti-union forces in Pueblo, Colorado, were behind the desecration. For months, the United Steelworkers had been engaged in a protracted strike against Rocky Mountain Steel Mills (a corporate descendant of Colorado Fuel and Iron) in Pueblo, and Ludlow had been a potent rallying cry among strikers. No arrests were ever made, and the UMWA joined with other unions to repair the statue. The

---

[7]Kenneth E. Foote, *Shadowed Ground: America's Landscape of Violence and Tragedy* (Austin: University of Texas Press, 1997), 300; Walker, "The Ludlow Massacre," 74.

[8]The term "wage-workers frontier" was coined by Carlos Schwantes; a good discus-sion of the concept appears in his "Wage Earners and Wealth Makers," in *The Oxford History of the American West*, ed. Clyde Milner, Carol O'Connor, and Martha A. Sandweiss, 431–67 (New York: Oxford University Press, 1994).

154

refurbished memorial was rededicated in a public ceremony in the spring of 2005. Once again, organized labor struggled to prevent the erasure of Ludlow from public memory.[9]

The very different positions that Ludlow and Johnson County occupy in public memory suggests that our notion of western violence has been shaped by a particular view of western history and the vaunted values of American freedom and independence. The feisty settlers of Johnson County who fought for their rights to the range and an independent livelihood reinforce Turner's view of the West as a land of freedom and opportunity. By contrast, the bloody mining wars of Colorado and other western mining districts suggest a view of the West that was far more oppressive and rife with inequality. This is not an uplifting or comforting version of western history; hence American popular culture has relentlessly promoted the Turnerian version while obscuring the more complex dynamics of race, class, and capitalist incorporation.

Remembering the workers' frontier—be it on the Wyoming range or in the Colorado coalfields—is critical to understanding the history of the American West. A full accounting of the ethnic, racial, gender, and class conflicts that shaped western violence enables us to come to grips with the more complicated story of western expansion, settlement, and incorporation. This is a history that continues to be relevant today. Changing environmental conditions and meat industry practices on the Great Plains, new energy demands and mining practices in the Rocky Mountains, and a renewed influx of immigrants into the western workforce all suggest that the history of western range and mining wars has implications for the region's present and future.

---

[9]James Green, "Crime against Memory at Ludlow," *Labor: Studies in Working Class History of the Americas*, 1 (Winter 2004): 9–16.

(opposite) **Figure 6.** *Vandalism in Ludlow*

In 2003, the eighty-five-year-old Ludlow memorial erected by the United Mine Workers was vandalized, leaving the statues of a miner and his wife decapitated. The union raised funds to repair the monument and rededicated it in 2005.

Courtesy of Dean Saitta.

A Chronology of the Johnson County War (1879–1893)

1879 Cattlemen bring first large herds of beef cattle into Johnson County; Wyoming Stock Growers Association (WSGA) organized in Cheyenne.

1884 WSGA pushes first maverick bill through territorial legislature, prohibiting mavericking and requiring WSGA branding and sale of mavericks; proceeds from sales used to hire stock detectives.

1885–1886 Large stock owners institute layoffs and wage cuts; cowboys go on strike in protest. WSGA prohibits stock owning by cowboys.

1886–1887 Disastrous winter kills thousands of cattle and puts many operators in debt or out of business.

1889 James Averell and Ellen Watson lynched near Sweetwater River.

1890 Wyoming becomes a state.

1891 Second antimavericking bill passed, authorizing Wyoming Livestock Commission to seize and impound cattle of suspected rustlers; five railroad carloads of cattle seized that fall.

Small cattle operators in Johnson County found Northern Wyoming Farmers and Stock Growers Association; declare intent to have separate roundup in April, a month before WSGA roundup.

Two supporters of new association, Orley E. "Ranger" Jones and John A. Tisdale, shot outside Buffalo; stock detective Frank Canton identified by eyewitness but not prosecuted.

1892 Hired gunmen recruited in Texas for WSGA; travel to Cheyenne, where they are joined by cattlemen and continue on to Casper and Johnson County; called "regulators."

April 9: Shoot-out at KC Ranch; Nate Champion and Nick Ray killed.

April 10: Regulators take refuge at TA Ranch.

April 11: Settlers arrive at TA Ranch, and fighting begins.

April 13: Sixth Cavalry dispatched from Fort McKinney to TA Ranch; regulators surrender and are taken to Fort McKinney.

April 17: Prisoners moved to Fort D. A. Russell outside Cheyenne.

May: Repeated outbreaks of violence against large ranchers in Johnson County; U.S. deputy marshal aligned with stock growers murdered.

Early June: At request of WSGA ranchers and Wyoming officials, President Benjamin Harrison dispatches Ninth Cavalry buffalo soldiers to Suggs, Wyoming.

June 17: Gunfight between white settlers and black troops in Suggs; one soldier killed and two others wounded.

August 10: Regulators freed on their own recognizance pending trial.

November: Democrats opposed to Johnson County invasion defeat incumbent Republicans Amos Barber for governor and Francis Warren and Joseph Carey for U.S. Senate.

1893   *January 2*: Trial of regulators set to begin but cases dismissed.

A Chronology of the Colorado Coal Strike (1913–1918)

1913   *July*: United Mine Workers of America (UMWA) dispatches forty-two organizers to southern Colorado coalfields to begin unionization campaign.

August 16: UMWA organizer Gerald Lippiatt killed by Baldwin-Felts Agency detective; killing spurs union organizing.

September 15–17: UMWA holds convention in Trinidad; Mother Jones addresses miners, who approve strike resolutions.

September 23: Strike begins.

October 17: Mine guards using armored car and machine guns attack Forbes camp; one striker killed, and a boy and a mine guard wounded.

October 24: Strikers, strikebreakers, and mine guards clash in Walsenburg; four strikers killed.

October 25: Strikers shoot a mine guard who tries to stop them from dynamiting a bridge near Primero Mine.

October 29: Governor Elias Ammons declares martial law and sends Colorado National Guard, under General John Chase, to coalfields.

November 8: Strikers ambush and kill three mine guards and a strikebreaker.

November 26: Governor Ammons rescinds order barring strikebreakers; National Guard begins escorting strikebreakers into mines.

December: Louis Tikas and other strike leaders arrested and jailed. Colorado State Federation of Labor holds hearings on brutality and civil rights abuses by National Guard.

1914   *January*: State Federation of Labor issues report and makes recommendations that Ammons ignores.

January 4–12: Mother Jones sets out from Denver for Trinidad but is arrested and sent back. She sneaks back into Trinidad and is arrested and jailed incommunicado for nine weeks in San Rafael Hospital outside town.

January 22: Women march in Trinidad to protest jailing of Mother Jones; disorder ensues, and mounted National Guard troops ride down protesters.

March 16: Mother Jones released from prison and sent out of strike zone; returns a week later and is arrested and imprisoned in basement cell of Walsenburg jail.

April: Governor Ammons withdraws bulk of National Guard troops; two companies remain, most of whom are Colorado Fuel and Iron (CFI) employees and mine guards.

April 19: Miners celebrate Greek Easter at Ludlow; armed soldiers ride into camp, and a hostile exchange follows.

April 20–21: Shots fired near Ludlow unleash a daylong battle between strikers and National Guard troops; by evening, most tents burned to the ground, and at least seven people lay dead, including three strike leaders. The next day, the dead bodies of two women and eleven children recovered in a pit under one of the tents.

April 22: UMWA issues call to arms to strikers, who are joined by hundreds of labor sympathizers from around the region.

Late April: Protest meetings held in Denver and other cities; strikers attack mines and company facilities in southern Colorado; more than thirty people killed.

Governor Ammons appoints special board of National Guard officers to report on Ludlow.

April 28: President Woodrow Wilson sends federal troops to Colorado at Governor Ammons's request; cease-fire arranged.

May: U.S. Commission on Industrial Relations begins hearings on Ludlow.

December 10: UMWA calls off strike.

1915 *May*: UMWA leader John Lawson found guilty of 1913 killing of a deputy and gets life sentence; conviction later overturned.

John D. Rockefeller Jr. begins public relations campaign to improve CFI's image; travels to Colorado, visits miners, and touts new Colorado Industrial Representation Plan.

1918 UMWA dedicates memorial to fallen miners at Ludlow.

Questions for Consideration

1. What beliefs and practices contributed to the rise of the cattle boom in the western plains states? Why did the cattle industry fall on such hard times by the mid-1880s, and how did the crisis affect stock growers and their employees?

2. How did the practice of mavericking evolve? How did different westerners define *rustling*, and why did the contested meaning of the term provoke such violent passions? What does the dispute over rustling suggest about the larger conflict over western lands and resources?

3. What factors led to the lynching of James Averell and Ellen Watson in 1889? How did ranchers such as John Clay (Document 7) justify the use of extralegal violence? Why did a woman like Watson become a victim, and what role did gender play in her treatment?

4. How did *Chicago Herald* reporter Sam Clover portray the regulators and their opponents during the Johnson County War (Document 9)? How does his style of writing compare with newspaper journalism today? Why would such a story have appealed to readers in Chicago?

5. Would you define the regulators as vigilantes or state-sanctioned actors? What role did state and federal authorities play in the Johnson County War and its aftermath, and whose interests did they serve?

6. Why were the regulators eventually exonerated? What does this case and others referred to in these documents suggest about the role of the justice system in Wyoming?

7. Compare the roles of the buffalo soldiers sent into Johnson County in June 1892 and the immigrant strikebreakers brought into Colorado mining towns in the early twentieth century. In what ways did race and ethnicity influence their plight?

8. What did the U.S. Commission on Industrial Relations see as the causes of the 1913–1914 Colorado coal strike (Document 18)? How did officials of Colorado Fuel and Iron defend their labor policies (Document 19)? How might this conflict have differed from other industrial disputes back east?

9. What was the relationship between the mine owners, union, and state government? How does this compare to that between the cattle owners, settlers, and state officials in Wyoming? How would you compare the federal government's role in these two conflicts?

10. How did the presence of the National Guard affect life in the strike zone? Why were the troops unable to stem the violence?

11. Why was Mother Jones so intent on returning to the strike zone? How did she cultivate her persona as a strike leader?

12. What role did women play in the strike? What do you make of the accounts of the women's march of January 22, 1914? Were these women active agents in the violence or merely victims of it?

13. The military called the events of April 20, 1914, the "Battle of Ludlow," while strikers dubbed it the "Ludlow Massacre." Was it, in your view, a battle or a massacre?

14. How did John D. Rockefeller Jr. hope to ameliorate industrial conflict in the wake of the strike (Document 30)? How viable was Rockefeller's vision of labor-management cooperation under the Colorado Industrial Representation Plan?

15. How well do the Johnson County War and the Colorado coal strike fit Richard Maxwell Brown's model of the "western civil wars of incorporation"? Which side, if any, won each of these wars and why?

16. Was there a point in each conflict when violence became unavoidable, and if so, when? If deadly violence was not inevitable, why did people choose to engage in it?

17. Why have ideas and images about western violence been so pervasive in American popular culture? How have the Johnson County War and Ludlow Massacre been remembered by later generations, and why has the former gotten so much more attention than the latter?

Selected Bibliography

GENERAL WORKS

Brown, Richard Maxwell. *No Duty to Retreat: Violence and Values in American History and Society.* New York: Oxford University Press, 1991.
———. *Strain of Violence: Historical Studies of American Violence and Vigilantism.* New York: Oxford University Press, 1975.
———. "Western Violence: Structure, Values, and Myth." *Western Historical Quarterly* 24 (February 1993): 4–20. Another version of this article appears under the title "Violence," in *The Oxford History of the American West,* edited by Clyde Milner, Carol O'Connor, and Martha A. Sandweiss, 393–425. New York: Oxford University Press, 1994.
Courtwright, David T. *Violent Land: Single Men and Social Disorder from the Frontier to the Inner City.* Cambridge, Mass.: Harvard University Press, 1996.
Dykstra, Robert R. "Violence, Gender, and Methodology in the 'New' Western History." *Reviews in American History* 27 (March 1999): 79–86.
McGrath, Roger. *Gunfighters, Highwaymen, and Vigilantes: Violence on the Frontier.* Berkeley: University of California Press, 1984.
McKanna, Clare V. *Homicide, Race, and Justice in the American West, 1880–1920.* Tucson: University of Arizona Press, 1997.
Pfeifer, Michael J. *Rough Justice: Lynching and American Society, 1894–1947.* Urbana: University of Illinois Press, 2004.
Rosenbaum, Robert J. *Mexicano Resistance in the Southwest.* Austin: University of Texas Press, 1981.
Slotkin, Richard. *The Fatal Environment: The Myth of the Frontier in the Age of Industrialization, 1800–1890.* New York: Atheneum, 1985.
Udall, Stewart. "The 'Wild' Old West: A Different View." *Montana* 49 (Winter 1999): 64–71.

JOHNSON COUNTY WAR

Belgrad, Daniel. "'Power's Larger Meaning': The Johnson County War as Political Violence in an Environmental Context." *Western Historical Quarterly* 33 (Summer 2002): 159–77.

Canton, Frank. *Frontier Trails: The Autobiography of Frank M. Canton.* 1930. Reprint, Norman: University of Oklahoma Press, 1966.

Clay, John. *My Life on the Range.* 1924. Reprint, Norman: University of Oklahoma Press, 1962.

Clover, Sam. "Regulators in a Trap." *Chicago Herald,* April 16, 1892.

DeArment, Robert K. *Alias Frank Canton.* Lincoln: University of Nebraska Press, 1996.

Downing, Ariel A. "Music as Artifact: The Johnson County War Ballads." *Annals of Wyoming* 70 (Winter 1998): 13–24.

Drago, Harry Sinclair. *The Great Range Wars: Violence on the Grasslands.* Lincoln: University of Nebraska Press, 1970.

Flagg, Oscar H. *A Review of the Cattle Business in Johnson County, Wyoming, since 1882, and the Causes That Led to the Recent Invasion.* 1892. Reprint, New York: Arno Press, 1969.

Hufsmith, George. *The Wyoming Lynching of Cattle Kate, 1889.* Glendo, Wyo.: High Plains Press, 1993.

McDermott, John D. "Writers in Judgment: Historiography of the Johnson County War." *Annals of Wyoming* 65 (Winter 1993–1994): 20–34.

Mercer, Asa Shinn. *The Banditti of the Plains.* 1894. Reprint, Norman: University of Oklahoma Press, 1954.

O'Neal, Bill. *The Johnson County War.* Austin, Tex.: Eakin Press, 2004.

Schubert, Frank N. "The Suggs Affray: The Black Cavalry in the Johnson County War." *Western Historical Quarterly* 4 (January 1973): 57–68.

Smith, Helena Huntington. *The War on Powder River.* New York: McGraw-Hill, 1966.

Woods, Lawrence M. *Asa Shinn Mercer: Western Promoter and Newspaperman, 1839–1917.* Spokane, Wash.: Clark, 2003.

———. *British Gentlemen in the Wild West: The Era of the Intensely English Cowboy.* New York: Free Press, 1989.

LUDLOW MASSACRE

Adams, Graham, Jr. *Age of Industrial Violence, 1910–1915.* New York: Columbia University Press, 1966.

Andrews, Thomas. "'Made by Toile': Tourism, Labor, and the Construction of the Colorado Landscape, 1858–1917." *Journal of American History* 92 (December 2005): 837–63.

Colorado Adjutant General. "Ludlow: Being the Report of the Special Board of Officers Appointed by the Governor of Colorado to Investigate and Determine the Facts with Reference to the Armed Conflict between the Colorado National Guard and Certain Persons Engaged in the Coal Mining Strike at Ludlow, Colorado, April 20, 1914." Denver, 1914.

Colorado State Federation of Labor. "Militarism in Colorado: Report of the Committee Appointed at the Suggestion of the Governor of Colorado to

Investigate the Conduct of the Colorado National Guard during the Coal Strike of 1913–1914." Denver, 1914.

Gitelman, Howard. *Legacy of the Ludlow Massacre: A Chapter in American Industrial Relations.* Philadelphia: University of Pennsylvania Press, 1988.

Gorn, Elliott J. *Mother Jones: The Most Dangerous Woman in America.* New York: Hill & Wang, 2001.

Green, James. "Crime against Memory at Ludlow." *Labor: Studies in Working Class History of the Americas* 1 (Winter 2004): 9–16.

Jones, Mother. *The Autobiography of Mother Jones.* 1925. Reprint, Chicago: Kerr, 1976.

Long, Priscilla. *Where the Sun Never Shines: A History of America's Bloody Coal Industry.* New York: Paragon House, 1989.

Margolis, Eric. "Mining Photographs: Unearthing the Meaning of Historical Photos." *Radical History Review* 40 (January 1988): 33–48.

Martelle, Scott. *Blood Passion: The Ludlow Massacre and Class War in the American West.* New Brunswick, N.J.: Rutgers University Press, 2007.

McGovern, George, and Leonard Guttridge. *The Great Coalfield War.* Boston: Houghton Mifflin, 1972.

O'Neal, Mary Thomas. *Those Damn Foreigners.* Hollywood, Calif.: Minerva Book, 1971.

Papanikolas, Zeese. *Buried Unsung: Louis Tikas and the Ludlow Massacre.* Salt Lake City: University of Utah Press, 1982.

Rudd, Sarah M. "Harmonizing *Corrido* and Union Song at the Ludlow Massacre." *Western Folklore* 61 (2002): 21–42.

Saitta, Dean, Mark Walker, and Paul Reckner. "Battlefields of Class Conflict: Ludlow Then and Now." *Journal of Conflict Archaeology* 1 (2005): 197–213.

Stein, Leon, and Philip Taft, eds. *Massacre at Ludlow: Four Reports.* New York: Arno Press, 1971.

U.S. Commission on Industrial Relations. *Final Report and Testimony.* Vols. 7–9. Washington, D.C., 1916.

U.S. Congress. House Committee on Mines and Mining. *Conditions in the Coal Mines of Colorado.* Washington, D.C., 1914.

Walker, Mark. "The Ludlow Massacre: Class, Warfare, and Historical Memory in Southern Colorado." *Historical Archaeology* 37 (Fall 2003): 66–80.

West, George P. U.S. Commission on Industrial Relations. *Report on the Colorado Strike.* Washington, D.C., 1915.

Zinn, Howard. "The Colorado Coal Strike, 1913–1914." In *Three Strikes: Miners, Musicians, Salesgirls, and the Fighting Spirit of Labor's Last Century,* edited by Howard Zinn, Dana Frank, and Robin D. G. Kelley, 7–55. Boston: Beacon Press, 2001.

FILMS

Heaven's Gate. 1980. DVD, MGM, 2000.
Johnson County War. DVD, Lions Gate, 2002.
Shane. 1953. DVD, Paramount Home Video, 2000.
The Virginian. 1929. VHS, KVC Entertainment, 1989.

MUSIC

Woody Guthrie. "Ludlow Massacre." 1944. The song can be heard on *Woody Guthrie: The Asch Recordings.* Vol. 3, *Hard Travelin'.* Smithsonian Folkways, 1999.

Acknowledgments (continued from p. iv)

Document 1: Walter Baron Von Richthofen, *Cattle Raising on the Plains of North America.* With an introduction by Edward Everett Dale. Norman: University of Oklahoma Press, 1885.

Document 3: Frank M. Canton, *Frontier Trails: The Autobiography of Frank M. Canton.* Edited by Edward Everett Dale. Norman: University of Oklahoma Press, 1930.

Document 6: John H. Fales, *Neither of Them Ever Stole a Cow.* Casper College Western History Center.

Document 16: "The Invasion Song," in Olive Wooley Burt, *American Murder Ballads and their Stories.* Oxford University Press, 1958. By permission of Oxford University Press, Inc.

Document 22: Mother Jones, *In Rockefeller's Prisons.* Charles H. Kerr, Chicago.

Index

Abilene, Texas, cattle town of, 10
adoption of white orphans by Mexican
     families, 6
"Affidavit Given to the Commission on
     Industrial Relations" (Snyder),
     133–34
African Americans, Ninth Calvary and, 9,
     17, 73–76
     "agitators," 86, 92–93, 96, 117
agrarian populists, struggle with capitalist
     interests, 8–9
agricultural workers
     IWW campaign against, 29
     union organization and, 31
Aguilar, tent camps in, 25
Alamo, 3
alcohol use, 4
American Legion members attack
     Wobblies, 29–30
Ammons, Governor Elias, 25–28, 96, 97,
     98f, 106, 113, 115
Anaconda, 19
Anglo homesteaders, capitalist development
     and violence with, 8–9
Angus, W. H. (Red Angus), 45–46, 58, 64,
     66, 81
anthracite coal mines, 22–23
anticapitalists, 9
anti-incorporation viewpoint, 148
Arapaho, massacre along Sand Creek, 3
arson, rates of, 5
Atlantic Monthly, 138
Aurora, gold mining town, homicide rates
     in, 4
Averell, James, 14, 15, 50–54, 56, 58, 156

Baldwin-Felts Agency, 25, 82
ballads, 80–91, 146
Baltimore, murder rates in, 4
banditry, organized, 2
"Banditti of the Plains, The" (Mercer),
     56–58, 76

Barber, Governor Amos, 16, 17, 58, 68, 78,
     157
Basch, Charles, 57–58
Basques, as sheep owners, 17
"Battle of Ludlow, The" (Colorado Adjutant
     General), 115–23
Baxter, George, 44
Bennett, Alvin, 79
Berdiker, Colonel, 109–10
Billy the Kid, 6
Bisbee, Arizona, violence against IWW
     strikers in, 29
bituminous coal reserves, 22
Blackfeet, massacre along Marias River, 3
Black Hand, fear of, 94
blacklist, 84
Blair, Henry, 44
Bodie, gold mining town, homicide rates
     in, 4
Bothwell ranch, 52–53
Boughton, Major Edward, 101, 115
boundary markers, sheepherders and, 17
Bowers, L. M., 85–86, 85n, 93–97
Bozeman Trail, 13
Brake, Edwin V., 95, 95n
branding, 44, 47, 54, 156
Brewster, Professor James, 99, 104
British Isles
     cattle investors from, 13
     vigilante tradition in, 7
brothel, frontier, 50, 50n2
Brown, Robert Maxwell, 8
brutality
     Colorado National Guard and, 99
     state-sanctioned war against Native
          Americans, 8
Buchanan, 50–51, 54
Buffalo, frontier town, 13, 16
Buffalo Bulletin, 47
buffalo hunting grounds for Lakota Sioux,
     12–13
buffalo soldiers, 17, 73–76, 157

167